Thai Cookbook

with Pictures

Simple & Delicious Thai Food Recipes for Beginners and Advanced Users

Martha Highfill

Table of Contents

Foreword

Crafting and designing a cookbook that explores the wonderful flavors of Thai cuisine isn't an easy task. Thai dishes are mostly made of a pretty complex array of ingredients that seems to mix all together to give an explosion of flavor with every bite! Just a single missing ingredient could drastically alter the flavor and create something unappealing and disappointing.

I strongly believe that the author of this book is himself a pretty strong and experience home chef because all of the recipes in this book are fool-proof and written to perfection. While I wasn't able to try all of them, the ones I did indeed give me a taste of the most authentic Thai tradition there is.

The recipes of this book work on many levels to perfectly capture the magical essence that makes Thai cuisine so special and delicate!

After going through so many cookbooks myself and trying to find out the perfect one that fully encapsulates Thai in its entirety, I think I found the one that I love. And that is the reason why I dedicate my time to writing a foreword for this particular book.

While trying some of the most classic and traditional Thai recipes available in this book, my husband instantly became irresistible to my cooking. My kids seem to love it.

I thank the author for producing such an amazing compilation. I hope to see more similar books in the future!

The strength of a successful cookbook lies in its ability to convey expert information to beginners in easily digestible chunks. They, like real cookbooks, are intended for people who might understand the theory or fundamentals of the challenge but lack the expertise and experience that an expert steeped in the technology would have. The cookbook encourages readers to practice and participate in expert practices to correctly teach them how to do the trade tricks.

Hopefully, this book will do the same for people who are just getting started on their first journey towards becoming a Thai culinary expert and help home chefs, both novice and advanced alike.

Alisha Patel

Sous Chef at Western Cuisine, Dhaka

Thai cuisine has a very infamous reputation for being extremely spicy! However, the reality is far from it.

Thai foods actually represent a very interesting and delicate balance between a multitude of flavors that beautifully blends the like of sourness, spiciness, saltiness, sweetness, and bitterness to create a carnival of flavors in your taste buds.

These flavors work to complement each other and create an immaculate meal that boasts a wide array of complex and mouthwatering flavor profiles that can easily hypnotize anyone who is having Thai.

In fact, a very well-known author and chef, Thompson, has creatively expressed his thoughts regarding Thai cuisine by saying that "Thai is such a cuisine that can be easily distinguished even from its nearest neighbors it terms flavors."

The ever-increasing number of Thai restaurants is a testament to Thai food's success, as more people remember the delicious mouth-tingling delights of authentic Thai cuisine.

Thai (Tai) people were originally refugees from southwest China who settled in the north and then moved south, establishing capitals with romantic names like Sukhothai ("Dawn of Happiness"), Ayutthaya ("Unassailable"), and then Bangkok ("City of Angels") at the end of the eighteenth century. As they moved south, they discovered that the fertile central plains and abundant rainfall were ideal for high-quality paddy fields, which is why the region is known as Southeast Asia's rice bowl.

Thailand is about the size of France and has a population of about 60 million people. Its immediate neighbors are Myanmar, Laos, Cambodia, and Malaysia. Many ingredients are similar to each cuisine but are often used in entirely different cooking methods due to trade between these and other countries in the region, conveniently illustrating the argument that food has no borders or boundaries. While regional cooking exists in Thailand, Thai restaurants will typically prepare and serve well-known dishes that they know their customers will enjoy.

Thai cuisine's evolution has been a long and subtle phase, with historical and culinary influences from China. Thais adopted dry spices — coriander, cumin, nutmeg, cloves, and turmeric — from Arab and Indian traders, as used in Thai Mussaman Curry. This added a new dimension to the work of the royal household's talented chefs, which gradually evolved into one of the world's most thrilling cuisines. The chili, which was carried east by the Portuguese, was perhaps the most important import. Its place in Thai cooking is undeniable, but it is the clever way the various flavors are married together to distinguish Thai cuisine. Threads of Indian cuisine can also be found in Thai cuisine's rich tapestry. The wet spice pastes are reminiscent of southern Indian masalas, which invariably contain the three Cs of oriental cooking: coconut, chili, and coriander/cilantro.

Thai food's three main draws are its flavors, textures, and aromas. Red and green hot bird's eye chilies; creamy coconut; coriander/cilantro (roots, stalks, and leaves); basil leaves, with their aniseed aroma; heavenly lemon grass; pine-like galangal (Kha); torn lime leaves (just smell the citrus fragrance); limes for juice or wedges to squeeze over prepared dishes; pungent kapi (fermented shrimp paste), which has no fishy taste but GI crisp green vegetables and unripe fruits for salads, such as green mango, meltingly tender deep-fried fish and curried meats, and juicy, simply prepared oriental fruits, such as mangosteens and lychees, are among the textures. The aroma of lemongrass and lime leaves, or the scent of curry paste mixed into coconut milk, is enough to whet the appetite.

A passion for food is a never-ending journey of discovery. There is always something different around the corner. With the popularity of Thai cuisine, the ingredients are becoming more readily available, whether in supermarkets or corner shops, so you, too, can cook authentic Thai food with the aid of these recipes.

This book aims all the very best and top Thai recipes are included in this book and much more!

Thai Donuts (Pa Thong Ko)

Preparation Time: 2 hours 10 minutes
Cooking Time: 10 minutes
Servings: 2
Ingredients:
- 2 cups flour
- ¼ teaspoon baking soda
- 2 teaspoons active dry yeast
- 2 teaspoons sugar
- 1 cup water
- ½ teaspoon salt
- Oil, for frying

Preparation:
1. In a large bowl. combine together the yeast, baking flour, sugar, and salt until mix well.
2. Then pour slowly water and mix to form a dough.
3. Knead the dough until al dente and then use a damp cloth to cover. Set aside for about 2 hours.
4. Divide the dough into little doughs and form them into 2-inch sticks. Then press in the center.
5. While pressing, in a pan, heat up the cooking oil and then add the donut inside.
6. Cook the donut until puffy and golden brown.
7. When cooked, remove from the pan and set it on a kitchen paper to drain the excess oil.
8. Serve and enjoy!

Serving Suggestions: Top with chocolate syrup before serving.
Variation Tip: Add cinnamon to enhance taste.
Nutritional Information per Serving:
Calories: 542 | Fat: 8.2g|Sat Fat: 1.1g|Carbs: 100.9g|Fiber: 4.2g|Sugar: 4.3g|Protein: 14.4g

Thai Pork Rice Porridge

Preparation Time: 15 minutes
Cooking Time: 1 hour 45 minutes
Servings: 6

Ingredients:
- 1 cup rice
- ⅛ pound ground pork
- 1 teaspoon fish sauce
- 1 egg
- ½ cup pork broth
- 1 clove garlic, diced
- Black pepper, to taste

Preparation:
1. In a pan, boil rice with the lid covered.
2. It takes about 90 minutes for the rice mixture simmering to form porridge like consistency. Stir occasionally.
3. In a large bowl, add garlic, ground pork, and fish sauce and mix well.
4. Form the mixture into bite-sized meatballs and set aside to later cooking.
5. Then add the pork broth, meatballs, and the black pepper together in the rice mixture and let it simmer for about 3 minutes.
6. Poach the eggs in the rice mixture until the egg white is formed.
7. When cooked, remove the congee from the pot and transfer into serving bowls. Serve and Enjoy!

Serving Suggestions: Top with scallion before serving.
Variation Tip: Fish sauce can be replaced with soy sauce.
Nutritional Information per Serving:
Calories: 141 | Fat: 1.4g|Sat Fat: 0.4g|Carbs: 25g|Fiber: 0.4g|Sugar: 0.2g|Protein: 6.1g

Spicy and Sour Thai Soft-Boiled Eggs

Preparation Time: 7 minutes
Cooking Time: 5 minutes
Servings: 4
Ingredients:
- 4 eggs
- 1 large lime
- 2 shallots, chopped
- 2 tablespoons fish sauce
- 1 teaspoon sugar
- 2 tablespoons chili flakes
- Salt, to taste

Preparation:
1. In a pan, add water and then bring to a boil. Add the whole eggs in the boiling water and simmer for about 5 minutes.
2. In a bowl, mix together the lime juice, fish sauce, sugar, chili flakes, and the chopped shallots.

Peel the eggs and cut into halves. Drizzle with sauce to serve. Enjoy! **Serving Suggestions:** Garnish with coriander before serving.
Variation Tip: You can also add cayenne pepper to enhance taste.
Nutritional Information per Serving:
Calories: 79 | Fat: 4.4g|Sat Fat: 1.4g|Carbs: 4.4g|Fiber: 0.5g|Sugar: 2g|Protein: 6.3g

Thai Pork Steamed Buns

Preparation Time: 2 hour 15 minutes
Cooking Time: 15 minutes
Servings: 12
Ingredients:
- 3¾ cups all-purpose flour
- ¼ cup caster sugar
- 4 tablespoons dry yeast
- ¾ cup water
- 3 tablespoons butter
- 1½ pounds minced pork
- ½ cup chopped spring onion
- 4 tablespoons oyster sauce
- 4 teaspoons sesame oil
- 4 garlic cloves
- 6 tablespoons soy sauce
- 2 teaspoons white pepper
- Pinch of salt
Preparation:
1. In a bowl, combine together the flour, yeast, and salt and properly sift. Then set aside until the yeast activates, for about 10 minutes.
2. Pour water into the flour mixture and mix to form a dough. Cover a damp cloth over. Allow it to sit for 45 minutes.
3. In a large bowl, mix together the minced pork, chopped garlic cloves, onion, oyster sauce, soy sauce, finely chopped white pepper, and sesame oil. Then refrigerate for about 1 hour.
4. Divide the dough into 24 pieces and flatten the pieces into circular shape. Ensure the edges are thinner than the center.
5. Then add the pork filling in the center of the dough. Wrap the bun.

6. Repeat with the remaining pieces and use a cloth to cover, about 15 minutes.
7. Steam for about 15 minutes.
8. When cooked, remove from the pot and serve warm.
9. Serve and enjoy!
Serving Suggestions: Serve with green chili sauce.
Variation Tip: You can add ginger powder in pork mixture.
Nutritional Information per Serving:
Calories: 685 | Fat: 12.7g|Sat Fat: 4.7g|Carbs: 72.9g|Fiber: 3.4g|Sugar: 4.7g|Protein: 65.6g

Classic Thai Grilled Chicken (Thai Gai Yang)

Preparation Time: 15 minutes
Cooking Time: 15 minutes
Servings: 3
Ingredients:
- ½ lemongrass stalk, chopped
- 1 shallot, chopped
- 1 tablespoon vegetable oil
- 2 tablespoons Thai thin soy sauce
- 1 tablespoon fish sauce
- 3 pounds chicken, cut into pieces
- ¼ cup cilantro, chopped
- 4 cloves garlic, chopped
- 1 tablespoon palm sugar
- 1 teaspoon Thai sweet soy sauce
- ¼ teaspoon turmeric powder
- Salt and black pepper, to taste
Preparation:
1. In a food processor, process together the lemongrass stalk, chopped shallot, vegetable oil, Thai thin soy sauce, fish sauce, chopped cilantro, chopped garlic cloves, palm sugar, Thai sweet soy sauce, turmeric powder, salt, and black pepper. Pulse several times to form a smooth mixture.
2. Coat the chicken pieces well with the sauce mixture and put in the refrigerator to marinade.
3. About 1 to 2 hours before cooking, take out the chicken and then set aside for later use.
4. Then grill the chicken about 15 minutes.
When cooked, serve in serving plates. Enjoy! **Serving Suggestions:** Serve with hot sauce.
Variation Tip: You can omit turmeric powder.
Nutritional Information per Serving:
Calories: 865 | Fat: 19g|Sat Fat: 4.8g|Carbs: 31.1g|Fiber: 0.2g|Sugar: 5.2g|Protein: 134.1g

Thai Shrimp Stuffed Waffles

Preparation Time: 10 minutes
Cooking Time: 15 to 20 minutes
Servings: 7
Ingredients:
- 2 tablespoons rice flour
- 3 tablespoons sugar
- 1 egg
- ¼ cup dried shrimp
- ½ cup all-purpose flour
- 6 tablespoons coconut milk
- ½ cup freshly squeezed lime juice

Preparation:
1. Prepare a waffle iron and grease evenly. Then heat before cooking begins.
2. In a large bowl. add sugar, egg, rice flour, dried shrimp, all-purpose flour, coconut milk, and lime juice and mix well until smooth.
3. Then pour the batter into the heated waffle iron. Cook for about 15 to 20 minutes.
4. When cooked, transfer to a serving plate and enjoy!

Serving Suggestions: Serve with maple syrup on the top.
Variation Tip: You can also add coriander leaves to enhance taste.
Nutritional Information per Serving:
Calories: 105 | Fat: 3.9g|Sat Fat: 3g|Carbs: 15.3g|Fiber: 0.6g|Sugar: 5.7g|Protein: 2.9g

Thai Fried Coconut Bananas

Preparation Time: 12 minutes
Cooking Time: 10 minutes
Servings: 10
Ingredients:
- 6 tablespoons white rice flour
- 1 tablespoon white sugar
- ¼ cup shredded coconut
- 5 bananas
- 2 tablespoons tapioca flour
- ½ cup water
- 1½ cups oil
- Salt, to taste

Preparation:
1. In a large bowl, add sugar, rice flour, shredded coconut, salt, and tapioca flour and drop a few water at a time. Mix well to form a thick batter.
2. Cut each banana into 3 to 4 slices and use the batter to cover the banana slices.
3. In a frying pan, heat the cooking oil and then add the covered bananas inside.
4. Fry the banana batters until golden.
5. Remove from the pan and serve.

Serving Suggestions: Top it with honey before serving.
Variation Tip: Use powdered cinnamon on the top.
Nutritional Information per Serving:
Calories: 1214 | Fat: 120.8g|Sat Fat: 16.2g|Carbs: 36.3g|Fiber: 2g|Sugar: 8.5g|Protein: 0.9g

Original Thai Omelet (Kai Jeow)

Prep Time: 10 minutes.
Cook Time: 5 minutes.
Serves: 4
Ingredients:
- 2 eggs
- ½ teaspoon fish sauce
- 2 sliced green onions
- 1 tablespoon vegetable oil

Preparation:
1. Green onions, thinly sliced in a mixing bowl, combine the eggs and fish sauce until frothy. Stir in the green onions.
2. In a small nonstick skillet, heat the oil over medium heat until it is very hot. Cook until the egg mixture is browned and crispy on the one hand, around 1-2 minutes.
3. Cook for another 1-2 minutes, or until the other side is browned, but the inside is still fluffy. (If you don't feel comfortable flipping the omelet all at once, fold it in half after about a minute and brown on both sides.)
4. If desired, serve with steamed jasmine rice and sriracha sauce.

Serving Suggestion: Serve over a bed of rice; you can go for sticky rice, jasmine rice, or any other rice appropriate for Thai cuisine. You may opt for Thai Fried Rice as well.
Variation Tip: Add banana blossom/basil/oyster sauce during or after cooking for an additional flavorful punch.
Nutritional Information Per Serving:
Calories 208 | Fat 15g |Sodium 347mg | Carbs 6g | Fiber 1g | Sugar 3g | Protein 12g

Thai Grilled Pork Kebabs

Preparation Time: 30 minutes
Cooking Time: 25 minutes
Servings: 6
Ingredients:
- ½ pound pork shoulder, cut into strips
- ½ lemongrass stalk, chopped
- 1½ tablespoons coconut milk
- ½ tablespoon light soy sauce
- 1 teaspoon vegetable oil
- 3 garlic cloves, peeled
- 1 tablespoon sugar
- 1 tablespoon fish sauce
- ½ tablespoon coriander stalk, roughly chopped

Preparation:
1. In a food processor, blend together the lemongrass, coconut milk, soy sauce, garlic cloves, sugar, vegetable oil, coriander stalk, and fish sauce. Pulse several times until a paste is formed.
2. Coat the pork strips with the paste and marinade in the refrigerator overnight.
3. Then thread the marinated pork strips on the skewers and set up the barbeque to grill the skewers directly.
4. When the coals turn white, grill the skewers and frequently turn to avoid burning until the skewers are cooked and caramelized.
5. It's time to treat yourself.

Serving Suggestions: Serve with your favored sauce.

Variation Tip: You can omit coriander stalk.

Nutritional Information per Serving:
Calories: 161 | Fat: 12.1g|Sat Fat: 6g|Carbs: 4.7g|Fiber: 0.3g|Sugar: 3.4g|Protein: 9.6g

Coconut Chicken Soup (Tom Khai Gai)

Prep Time: 15 minutes.
Cook Time: 20 minutes.
Serves: 4
Ingredients:
- ¾ pound boneless chicken meat
- 3 tablespoons vegetable oil
- 2 (14-ounce) cans coconut milk
- 2 tablespoons fresh ginger root, minced
- 4 tablespoons fish sauce
- ½ cup fresh lime juice
- ¼ teaspoon cayenne pepper
- ½ teaspoon ground turmeric
- 2 tablespoons scallions, sliced
- 1 tablespoon fresh cilantro, chopped

Preparation:
1. Cut up your chicken into strips.
2. Take a skillet and place it over medium heat, add oil, and heat it up.
3. Add the chicken strips and sauté them for about 2-3 minutes.
4. Take a pot and bring the coconut milk and water to a boil.
5. Lower down the heat to low.
6. Add ginger, lime juice, fish sauce, turmeric, and cayenne powder.
7. Simmer the chicken for about 10-15 minutes.
8. Sprinkle it with a bit of cilantro and scallions.
9. Serve hot!

Serving Suggestion: If possible, add a bit of cream on top before serving, and some mint on top.
Variation Tip: Add banana blossom/basil during or after cooking for an additional flavorful punch.
Nutritional Information Per Serving:
Calories 303 | Fat 21g |Sodium 662mg | Carbs 16g | Fiber 1g | Sugar 7g | Protein 15g

Refreshing Cucumber Soup

Prep Time: 15 minutes.
Cook Time: 30 minutes.
Serves: 4
Ingredients:
- 2 tablespoons butter
- 2 tablespoons green onion, sliced
- 3 cucumbers, chopped
- ⅓ cup red wine vinegar
- 1-quart chicken broth
- 2 cups water
- 3 hot chile peppers, minced and seeded
- 3 tablespoons fresh parsley, chopped
- 1 tablespoon fresh cilantro, chopped
- 1 tablespoon fish sauce
- 1 teaspoon soy sauce
- Salt as needed
- Pepper as needed
- ½ cup sour cream
- 2 white stalks of lemon grass, bruised
- 1 ½ inches ginger, sliced

Preparation:
1. Take a deep pan and place it over medium heat.
2. Add butter and allow it to heat up.
3. Add green onions and cook them until tender.
4. Stir in vinegar, cucumber, chicken broth, chile peppers, water, parsley, lemon grass, cilantro, garlic, soy sauce, fish sauce, ginger.
5. Season with some salt and pepper.
6. Simmer it over medium heat until the cucumbers are tender for about 20 minutes.
7. Stir in sour cream and simmer for 10 minutes more.
8. Enjoy!

Serving Suggestion: If possible, add a bit of cream.
Variation Tip: Add shredded coconut on top.
Nutritional Information Per Serving:
Calories 135 | Fat 8g |Sodium 655mg | Carbs 11g | Fiber 2g | Sugar 8g | Protein 5g

Hot and Sour Tom Yum Soup with Shrimp (Tom Yum Goong)

Prep Time: 10 minutes.
Cook Time: 5 minutes.
Serves: 4
Ingredients:
- 4 cups water or basic Thai chicken stock
- 6 (⅛-inch-thick) slices unpeeled fresh galangal, bruised with the butt of a chef's knife, optional

- 3 lemon grass stalks (bottom 3 inches only), bruised with the flat side of a chef's knife
- 2 fresh kaffir lime leaves, optional
- 2 tablespoons roasted chili paste
- 3 tablespoons fish sauce
- 1 cup fresh button mushrooms cut into ¼ -inch slices, or canned straw mushrooms, drained and halved or left whole
- 12 large raw shrimp, deveined, peeled, or impeded, as you prefer; if removing the shell, leave tails on for a nicer presentation
- ¼ cup lime juice, freshly squeezed
- 1 or 2 fresh red Thai bird's-eye chiles, stemmed, seeded, and each thinly sliced lengthwise into 4 strips, optional
- ¼ cup fresh cilantro leaves, for serving

Preparation:
1. Take a medium saucepan and add water, lemon grass, and kaffir lime leaves into it.
2. Cover and bring just to a boil over high heat.
3. Turn the heat to low and simmer for 5 minutes.
4. Remove and discard lemon grass and lime leaves.
5. Stir in the chili paste.
6. Add the mushrooms and simmer for 1 minute.
7. Then add the shrimp and simmer for 1 minute more.
8. Remove from the heat and stir in the lime juice and chiles.
9. Adjust the seasoning, as needed, with additional fish sauce or lime juice.
10. Take a small bowl and sprinkle with cilantro on top.
11. Serve and enjoy!

Serving Suggestion: Serve over a bed of rice; you can go for sticky rice, jasmine rice, or any other rice appropriate for Thai cuisine.
Variation Tip: Add banana blossom/basil/chili peppers during or after cooking for an additional flavorful punch.
Nutritional Information Per Serving:
Calories 167 | Fat 6g |Sodium 1429mg | Carbs 16g | Fiber 3g | Sugar 5g | Protein 14g

Thai Chicken Noodle Soup

Prep Time: 15 minutes.
Cook Time: 20 minutes.
Serves: 2
Ingredients:
- 4 ounces dry Chinese noodles
- 1 (14.5-ounce) can chicken broth
- 6 shitake mushrooms, sliced
- 2 green onions, chopped
- 1 skinless and boneless chicken breast half
- 2 eggs

Preparation:
1. Take a bowl of water and bring it to a boil.

2. Stir in noodles and cook until al dente for about 8-10 minutes.
3. Drain the noodles and divide them into two serving bowls.
4. Take a medium-sized saucepan and place it over medium heat.
5. Add chicken broth and bring it to a boil.
6. Add green onions and mushrooms.
7. Cut up the chicken into bite-sized portions and stir it into the broth.
8. Once the broth comes to a boil, crack in the eggs.
9. Keep cooking for about 10 minutes until the chickens are no longer pink, and the eggs are cooked.
10. Pour the chicken soup over the noodle bowls.
11. Enjoy!

Serving Suggestion: Add some crunchy noodle on top for additional crunch.
Variation Tip: Add cilantro/coriander/oyster sauce during or after cooking for an additional flavorful punch.
Nutritional Information Per Serving:
Calories 902 | Fat 56g |Sodium 1455mg | Carbs 29g | Fiber 5g | Sugar 5g | Protein 68g

Thai Shrimp Rice Soup

Preparation Time: 25 minutes
Cooking Time: 30 minutes
Servings: 8
Ingredients:
- 6 cups chicken stock
- ½ teaspoon white peppercorns
- ½ pound shrimp, cut into small chunks
- 1 tablespoon soy sauce
- 6 cups cooked jasmine rice
- 6 garlic cloves, minced
- 12 cilantro stems
- 2 tablespoons fish sauce

Preparation:
1. In a food processor, add the garlic, cilantro, and white peppercorns and pulse to form a smooth puree. Use half the puree to marinade shrimps.
2. Sauté the marinated shrimps in a pan and add chicken stock in it.
3. Bring to a boil and pour in the remaining puree in the pot, stirring continuously.
4. Then add rice and cook for about 5 minutes.
5. When cooked, remove from heat. Add fish sauce and soy sauce and stir well to combine.
6. Serve and enjoy!

Serving Suggestions: Top with coriander leaves before serving.
Variation Tip: Soy sauce can be omitted.
Nutritional Information per Serving:
Calories: 528 | Fat: 0.9g|Sat Fat: 0.3g|Carbs: 110.3g|Fiber: 6.2g|Sugar: 0.8g|Protein: 16.6g

Exotic Thai Pumpkin Soup

Prep Time: 10 minutes.
Cook Time: 15 minutes.
Serves: 4
Ingredients:
- 1 tablespoon vegetable oil
- 1 tablespoon butter
- 1 chopped garlic clove
- 4 chopped shallots
- 2 small-sized fresh red chili pepper, chopped up
- 1 tablespoon chopped lemon grass
- 2 ⅛ cups chicken stock
- 4 cups peeled and diced pumpkin
- 1 ½ cups unsweetened coconut milk
- 1 bunch fresh basil leaves

Preparation:
1. Take a medium-sized saucepan and place it over low heat.
2. Add oil and heat it up.
3. Add butter and melt.
4. Add garlic, chilies, shallots, lemon grass, and stir until fragrant.
5. Stir in chicken stock, pumpkin, and coconut milk.
6. Bring the mixture to a boil.
7. Cook until the pumpkin is tender.
8. Take a blender and blend the sup in batches until a smooth soup form.
9. Serve the soup with some basil leaves!

Serving Suggestion: Add a bit of cream before serving for added flavor.

Variation Tip: Add cilantro/coriander/oyster sauce during or after cooking for an additional flavorful punch.

Nutritional Information Per Serving:
Calories 268 | Fat 17g |Sodium 81mg | Carbs 29g | Fiber 2g | Sugar 14g | Protein 5g

Tom Yum Koon Soup

Prep Time: 15 minutes.
Cook Time: 40 minutes.
Serves: 4
Ingredients:
- ½ pound medium-sized peeled and deveined shrimp
- 12 mushrooms, halved
- 1 (4.5-ounce) can drained mushrooms
- 4 cups water
- 2 lemon grass
- 4 kaffir lime leaves
- 4 slices galangal
- 4 chile Padi
- 1 ½ tablespoons fish sauce
- Juice of 1 ½ limes
- 1 teaspoon white sugar
- 1 teaspoon hot chili paste
- 1 tablespoon tom yum sour paste, optional

Preparation:
1. Take a bowl and place it over medium-high heat.
2. Add shrimp heads and shells to water.
3. Cook for about 20 minutes.
4. Remove the heat.
5. Then soak the head and shells for about 20 minutes, discard them.
6. Trim the lemon grass and cut into matchstick size pieces.
7. Take a pot and add lemon grass, stock, kaffir lime leaves, chile Padi, lime juice, fish sauce, galangal, sugar, and chili paste.
8. Bring it to a boil and allow it to boil for 5 minutes.
9. Add shrimps and mushrooms.
10. Cook for 10 minutes more.
11. Garnish with some coriander leaves.
12. Enjoy!

Serving Suggestion: Serve over a bed of rice; you can go for sticky rice, jasmine rice, or any other rice appropriate for Thai cuisine.

Variation Tip: Add banana blossom /oyster sauce during or after cooking for an additional flavorful punch.

Nutritional Information Per Serving:
Calories 260 | Fat 9g |Sodium 1439mg | Carbs 18g | Fiber 3g | Sugar 3g | Protein 29g

Thai Red Curry Noodle Soup

Prep Time: 15 minutes.
Cook Time: 25 minutes.
Serves: 4
Ingredients:
- 1 tablespoon of olive oil
- 1 pound boneless, skinless chicken breast, cut into 1-inch chunks

- Kosher salt and freshly ground black pepper, to taste
- 3 minced garlic cloves
- 1 diced red bell pepper
- 1 diced onion
- 3 tablespoons red curry paste
- 1 tablespoon ginger, freshly grated
- 6 cups chicken broth (low sodium)
- 1 can (13.5 oz.) coconut milk
- ½ box (8 oz.) rice noodles
- 1 teaspoon fish sauce
- 2 tablespoons brown sugar
- 3 thinly sliced green onions
- ½ cup clean cilantro leaves, chopped
- ¼ cup organic basil leaves, chopped
- 2 tablespoons lime juice, freshly squeezed

Preparation:

1. In a big stockpot or Dutch oven, heat the olive oil over medium heat. Season the chicken to taste with salt and pepper. Cook the chicken in the stockpot until golden, about 2-3 minutes; set aside.
2. Mix in the garlic, bell pepper, and onion. Cook, stirring periodically, until the vegetables are tender, around 3-4 minutes.
3. Stir in the red curry paste and ginger for around 1 minute, or until fragrant.
4. Scrape any browned bits from the bottom of the pot and stir in the chicken broth and coconut milk.
5. Add the chicken and mix well. Bring to a boil; reduce heat and cook, stirring periodically, for 10 minutes, or until reduced.
6. Stir in the rice noodles, fish sauce, and brown sugar for about 5 minutes, or until the noodles are soft.
7. Remove from heat; stir in green onions, cilantro, basil, and lime juice; season to taste with salt and pepper.
8. Serve right away!

Serving Suggestion: Add some crumbled noodles on top; it will give an extra crunch.

Variation Tip: Add coriander/oyster sauce during or after cooking for an additional flavorful punch.

Nutritional Information Per Serving:

Calories 480 | Fat 10g | Sodium 1553mg | Carbs 72g | Fiber 15g | Sugar 15g | Protein 24g

Thai Coconut Mushroom Shrimp Soup

Preparation Time: 15 minutes
Cooking Time: 26 minutes
Servings: 4
Ingredients:
- ½ tablespoon vegetable oil

- ½ lemongrass stalk, minced
- 2 cups chicken broth
- ½ tablespoon brown sugar
- ¼ pound fresh shiitake mushrooms, sliced
- 1 tablespoon fresh lime juice
- 2 tablespoons fresh cilantro
- 1 tablespoon grated fresh ginger
- 1 teaspoon red curry paste
- 1½ tablespoons fish sauce
- 3 cups coconut milk
- ½ pound shrimp, peeled and deveined
- Salt, to taste

Preparation:

1. In a pan, add the vegetable oil and heat. When heated, add ginger, curry paste, and lemongrass and cook for about 1 minute, stirring to combine.
2. Then pour in fish sauce, chicken broth, and sugar. Simmer for about 15 minutes, stirring often.
3. Add mushrooms and the coconut milk and cook for about 5 minutes.
4. Then add shrimp and cook for 5 more minutes, stirring often.
5. Remove from heat. Add lime juice and salt and stir to combine.
6. Add cilantro to garnish.
7. Serve and enjoy!

Serving Suggestions: Top with shredded coconut before serving.

Variation Tip: You can use chili sauce to enhance taste.

Nutritional Information per Serving:

Calories: 557 | Fat: 46.8g | Sat Fat: 39g | Carbs: 19.5g | Fiber: 4.8g | Sugar: 9.6g | Protein: 21.3g

Thai Chicken Soup

Preparation Time: 15 minutes
Cooking Time: 40 minutes
Servings: 3
Ingredients:
- ½ (4 pounds) chicken, cut into pieces
- 2 thin slices of fresh ginger
- 1 cup fresh cilantro
- 1 tablespoon lime juice
- ½ tablespoon fish sauce
- 4 cups water
- 2 garlic cloves, smashed
- 1½ shallots, thinly sliced
- 1 lemongrass stalk, chopped
- 1 fresh green Thai chili, thinly sliced
- Salt, to taste

Preparation:

1. In a large pan, add the chicken pieces, water, and salt and bring to boil.

2. In the boiling water, add ginger, garlic, shallot slices, lemongrass, lime juice, and cilantro and stir well.

3. Reduce the heat to simmer for about 30 minutes.

4. Then strain the soup, while discard the solids.

5. In a skillet, pour in the soup. Add in the chili and fish sauce to season and simmer for about 10 minutes.

6. When cooked, remove from the skillet and serve in a serving bowl.

7. Serve and enjoy!

Serving Suggestions: Top with cilantro before serving.

Variation Tip: Fish sauce can be replaced with soy sauce.

Nutritional Information per Serving:
Calories: 129 | Fat: 1.5g|Sat Fat: 0.7g|Carbs: 20g|Fiber: 0.6g|Sugar: 1.4g|Protein: 9g

Thai Coconut Red Curry Rice Noodle Soup

Preparation Time: 10 minutes
Cooking Time: 20 minutes
Servings: 3
Ingredients:
- 1 tablespoon avocado oil
- ¼ cup diced red bell pepper
- 1½ garlic cloves, minced
- 2 tablespoons red curry paste
- 1 cup coconut milk
- ¼ cup rice noodles
- ¼ cup chopped cilantro
- ¼ cup diced yellow onion
- ¼ cup diced carrots
- ½ tablespoon freshly grated ginger
- 3 cups chicken broth
- 1½ tablespoons fish sauce
- ½ tablespoon fresh lime juice
- Salt and pepper, to taste

Preparation:
1. In a Dutch oven, add the avocado oil and heat. When heated, add the carrots, onions, and red bell pepper and cook for about 7 minutes.

2. Add ginger, garlic, and red curry paste, stirring. Cook for 1 minute.

3. Then stir in chicken broth, fish sauce, and coconut milk.

4. Season with salt and pepper and cook for about 5 minutes.

5. Add the rice noodles in the soup and simmer for about 7 minutes.

6. When cooked, remove from the oven and add lime juice and cilantro to serve.

Serving Suggestions: Serve with soy sauce.

Variation Tip: You can also use vinegar to enhance taste.

Nutritional Information per Serving:
Calories: 320 | Fat: 24.2g|Sat Fat: 18.4g|Carbs: 18.1g|Fiber: 3g|Sugar: 6.2g|Protein: 9.3g

Thai Pumpkin and Tofu Soup

Preparation Time: 8 minutes
Cooking Time: 10 minutes
Servings: 1
Ingredients:
- 3 cups chicken stock
- 1 garlic clove, minced
- ½ red chili pepper, sliced
- 1 cup yam, chopped
- ½ teaspoon ground coriander
- 1 tablespoon fish sauce
- ½ teaspoon brown sugar
- ½ cup coconut milk
- 2 tablespoons lemon grass, minced
- ½ shallot, minced
- 1½ cups pumpkin, peeled and cut into chunks
- ¼ teaspoon turmeric
- ½ teaspoon ground cumin
- ½ teaspoon shrimp paste
- 1 tablespoon lime juice
- 1 cup soft tofu, cubed

Preparation:
1. In a pan, pour in the chicken stock.

2. Then add chili, garlic, lemongrass, and shallot and bring together to a boil.

3. Add the yam and pumpkin in the boiling soup and cook for about 7 minutes.

4. Season with the spices and flavorings. Stir in ground cumin, fish sauce, shrimp paste, brown sugar, lime juice, and turmeric until mix well.

5. Simmer the mixture for a while and then add the coconut milk and tofu.

6. When cooked, remove from the pan and transfer to a serving bowl.

7. Serve and enjoy!

Serving Suggestions: You can serve with chopped cilantro on the top.

Variation Tip: You can also add spinach in the soup.

Nutritional Information per Serving:
Calories: 970 | Fat: 34.7g|Sat Fat: 27.9g|Carbs: 166.3g|Fiber: 47.6g|Sugar: 54.3g|Protein: 23.8g

Easy Vegan Tom Yum Soup

Preparation Time: 10 minutes
Cooking Time: 15 minutes
Servings: 2
Ingredients:
• 3 cups vegetable stock
• 1 lime leaf
• 2 garlic cloves, minced
• ½ cup fresh mushrooms, sliced
• ½ cup cherry tomatoes
• ½ teaspoon brown sugar
• ½ tablespoon fresh lime juice
• 1 lemongrass stalk, minced
• ½ red chili, sliced
• ½ ginger, sliced
• 1 cup chopped Bok choy leaves
• 1 tablespoon soy sauce
• 1 cup soft tofu, cubed
Preparation:
1. In a pot, add vegetable stock and heat. When heated, add lime leaf, garlic, ginger, lemongrass, and chili and stir well.
2. Then bring the mixture to a boil. Add mushrooms and simmer for about 8 minutes.
3. Add cherry tomatoes and Bok choy and simmer for about 2 minutes, stirring properly.
4. Season with sugar, soy sauce, and lime juice.
5. Then add tofu and stir well.
6. When prepared, remove the soup from the pot and transfer to a serving bowl.
7. Serve and enjoy!
Serving Suggestions: Top with chopped basil leaves before serving.
Variation Tip: Coconut milk can also be added in the soup.
Nutritional Information per Serving:
Calories: 150 | Fat: 5.5g|Sat Fat: 0.7g|Carbs: 18.2g|Fiber: 4.9g|Sugar: 6.1g|Protein: 13.7g

Thai Mushroom Pork Wonton Soup

Preparation Time: 10 minutes
Cooking Time: 15 minutes
Servings: 8
Ingredients:
• 4 tablespoons canola oil
• 4 cups water
• 4 garlic cloves, chopped
• 2 pounds ground pork
• 2 tablespoons soy sauce
• 4 tablespoons fresh lime juice
• 4 scallions, thinly sliced
• 2 tablespoons fresh ginger, chopped
• 1 pound shiitake mushrooms
• 8 cups low-sodium chicken broth
• 8 cups wonton wrappers, sliced into ½ inch strips
• Salt, to taste
Preparation:
1. In a pan, add oil and heat over medium-high heat.
2. Add in garlic, ginger, and scallion and cook until fragrant. Then add the pork in the pan and cook for 8 minutes.
3. Stir in mushrooms and add salt to season. Stir for about 3 minutes.
4. Pour in chicken broth, soy sauce, and water and bring all together to boil.
5. Stir in wonton wrappers and reduce heat to simmer in the pan for about 2 minutes.
6. Pour in the lime juice to season.
7. Remove from the pan and transfer to a serving bowl.
Serve and enjoy! **Serving Suggestions:** Serve with crackers.
Variation Tip: You can add chopped red pepper to add spicy taste.
Nutritional Information per Serving:
Calories: 380 | Fat: 11.7g|Sat Fat: 2g|Carbs: 31.5g|Fiber: 2.3g|Sugar: 2.7g|Protein: 36.4g

Nutritious Thai Vegetable Soup

Preparation Time: 20 minutes
Cooking Time: 30 minutes
Servings: 10
Ingredients:
• 3½ cups tofu, drained, pressed and sliced
• 2 carrots, chopped
• 4 tablespoons minced ginger
• 2 tablespoons minced garlic
• 8 cups vegetable broth
• 4 Bok choy heads, roughly chopped
• 6 tablespoons extra-virgin olive oil
• 2 onions, finely chopped

- 2 red bell peppers, thinly sliced
- 3 cups chopped mushrooms
- 4 tablespoons curry powder
- 2 tablespoons lemongrass paste
- 8 cups coconut milk
- ½ cup chopped basil leaves
- Salt, to taste

Preparation:
1. In a pot, add olive oil and heat. When heated, add tofu and cook for about 7 minutes.
2. Season with salt. Then remove from the pot and set aside for later use.
3. Add onions, peppers, and mushrooms in the pot. Cook for about 7 minutes, stirring occasionally.
4. Then add curry powder, garlic, ginger, lemongrass paste, and mushrooms. Cook for about 2 minutes and mix well.
5. Add coconut milk, vegetable broth, and tofu in the pot and simmer for 15 minutes.
6. When cooked, remove from the pot and transfer to a serving plate.
7. Garnish with basil on the top. Serve and enjoy!

Serving Suggestions: Serve with chopped mint leaves on the top.

Variation Tip: You can also use soy sauce to enhance taste.

Nutritional Information per Serving:
Calories: 908 | Fat: 72.9g|Sat Fat: 45.7g|Carbs: 34.8g|Fiber: 13.6g|Sugar: 16.7g|Protein: 47.2g

Thai Red Curry Butternut Squash Soup

Preparation Time: 20 minutes
Cooking Time: 30 minutes
Servings: 12
Ingredients:
- 4 tablespoons olive oil
- 2 yellow onions, chopped
- 6 tablespoons red curry paste
- 2 teaspoons ground cumin
- ¼ teaspoon red pepper flakes
- 8 cups vegetable broth
- 1 cup unsweetened coconut flakes
- 4 pounds butternut squash, cut into pieces
- 8 garlic cloves, chopped
- 4 teaspoons ground coriander
- 2 teaspoons lime juice
- Salt, to taste

Preparation:
1. In a pan, add olive oil and heat. When heated, add all the spices and the vegetables in the pan and cook for about 8 minutes.

2. Then add the red curry paste and cook for 1 minute.
3. Stir in broth and simmer for about 20 minutes. Add coconut flakes and stir well.
4. Remove from the pan and transfer to a serving bowl.
5. Drizzle with lime juice. Serve and enjoy!

Serving Suggestions: Garnish with red chili flakes before serving.

Variation Tip: Use oregano to enhance taste.

Nutritional Information per Serving:
Calories: 201 | Fat: 10.1g|Sat Fat: 3.4g|Carbs: 24.3g|Fiber: 4.2g|Sugar: 4.7g|Protein: 5.5g

Thai Coconut Tofu Soup

Preparation Time: 10 minutes
Cooking Time: 15 minutes
Servings: 8
Ingredients:
- 1 red onion, chopped
- 6 mushrooms, sliced
- 1-inch piece of ginger, peeled and finely chopped
- 4 cups vegetable broth
- 2 tablespoons brown sugar
- 2 tablespoons soy sauce
- 1 red bell pepper, chopped
- 4 garlic cloves, chopped
- 1 Thai chili, finely chopped
- 3½ cups coconut milk
- 2½ cups firm tofu, cubed
- 2 tablespoons lime juice

Preparation:
1. Add ginger, mushrooms, garlic, red bell pepper, onion, and Thai chili in a large pot.
2. Then stir in coconut milk and vegetable broth and mix in sugar.
3. Bring the mixture to a boil and boil for about 5 minutes over medium heat.
4. Add tofu and cook for 5 more minutes, stirring often.
5. Remove from heat. Add the soy sauce and lime sauce and stir well to combine.
6. Serve and enjoy!

Serving Suggestions: Top with chopped cilantro before serving.

Variation Tip: Soy sauce can be replaced with tamari.

Nutritional Information per Serving:
Calories: 1393 | Fat: 126.1g|Sat Fat: 101.3g|Carbs: 47.7g| Fiber: 14.1g|Sugar: 23.6g|Protein: 41.9g

Crispy Fluffy Fish and Mango (Yam Pla Dook Foo)

Prep Time: 15 minutes.
Cook Time: 20 minutes.
Serves: 4

Ingredients:

For the Mango Salad
- Thai chilies, to taste
- 2 tablespoons palm sugar, finely chopped
- 2 tablespoons fish sauce
- 2 tablespoons lime juice
- 12 thinly sliced shallot
- 1 tablespoon dried shrimp, diced
- 1 julienned sour green mango (see note)
- 2 tablespoons cilantro, chopped

For Fish
- ½ pound any kind of fish meat
- 1 teaspoon soy sauce or a pinch of salt
- 3 tablespoons roasted peanuts
- frying oil

Preparation:
1. Season the fish with soy sauce or salt and steam for 5 minutes or until the meat is completely cooked. If you don't want to steam the fish, you can cook it in whatever way you want as long as you don't get a browned crispy crust on it (poach, bake, even stir-fry in a pan on low heat). When done, allow the fish to cool so you can handle it more easily.
2. Make the mango salad while the fish is cooking and cooling. Pound the Thai chilies in a mortar until there are no more large chunks (chili skin is fine), then add the palm sugar and mash until it's a muddy paste. Swirl in the fish sauce and lime juice until the sugar is fully dissolved. Transfer to a mixing bowl and add the dried shrimp, shallots, and mango. Allow setting while you cook the fish.
3. When the fish has cooled enough to treat, place it in a muslin-lined tub. Wrap the cloth around the fish, twist it to hold the fish in the cloth, and squeeze as hard as you can to get rid of as much liquid as possible (this is why you should let the fish cool; if it's too warm, you won't want to squeeze as hard!).
4. Transfer the fish to a mortar and pestle, and pound it until soft and free of chunks.
5. Heat about 1 - 1.5 inch of oil in a wok or deep pot over high heat to 400°F, and please read and observe the safety precautions above! (Tip: It would be easier to fold the fish if you use a larger pot or wok for this since you will be able to get to it more quickly. Note: For the amount specified in this recipe, you can make two batches of fried fish in a 9-inch-diameter pot.)

6. When the oil reaches temperature, add about half of the fish, and the oil will bubble vigorously. Push the edges of the fish in with a skimmer to clean them up, then leave the fish to fry until golden. I like to force the fish down every now and then so the top is submerged, which helps the fish brown more uniformly. When the fish is golden brown, you can fold it over into a half circle or any shape you like, but this is not needed. Take the fish from the oil with a slotted skimmer and shake it several times to extract the oil that has become trapped inside the fish until the bubbling has slowed and the fish is golden all over. Set aside on a paper towel to drain.
7. Arrange the fish on a plate and top with roasted peanuts. Serve the mango salad alongside the tuna, garnished with chopped cilantro. With jasmine rice, serve. Have fun!

Serving Suggestion: Serve over a bed of rice; you can go for sticky rice, jasmine rice, or any other rice appropriate for Thai cuisine.

Variation Tip: Add coriander/oyster sauce during or after cooking for an additional flavorful punch.

Nutritional Information Per Serving:
Calories 351 | Fat 26g |Sodium 372mg | Carbs 29g | Fiber 7g | Sugar 16g | Protein 7g

Authentic Seafood Platter (Yam Talay)

Prep Time: 15 minutes.
Cook Time: 10-15 minutes.
Serves: 4

Ingredients:

For seafood
- 24 small mussels
- 1 tablespoon table salt
- ¾ pound medium (51 to 60 per lb.) new peeled and deveined shrimp
- ½ pound washed squid, sliced crosswise into ¼-inch circles, tentacles cut in half if wide
- ½ pound sea scallops or bay scallops
- ¼ pound jumbo lump crabmeat, fresh or pasteurized

To make the dressing:
- 6 tablespoons new lime juice (from 2 limes)
- 4 ½ tablespoons fish sauce
- 1 ½ tablespoons granulated sugar
- 2 teaspoons finely chopped unseeded fresh hot green chiles (such as serrano or jalapeno)
- 2 tablespoons finely chopped garlic (2 medium cloves)

To make the salad:
- 2 cups rinsed and spun-dry bite-size Boston lettuce (1 large head)
- 3 tablespoons thinly sliced shallot (1 large)

- ⅓ cup scallions, thinly sliced (4 to 5, white and green parts)
- ¼ cup fresh cilantro, coarsely chopped
- ¼ cup new mint, coarsely chopped
- ½ cup sliced English cucumber (cut cucumber in half lengthwise and slice into ¼-inch thick half-moons)
- ½ cup cherry or grape tomatoes, halved

Preparation:

1. Scrub the mussels thoroughly under running water and remove any "beards." Any mussels that do not close tightly when tapped on the counter should be discarded.
2. In a medium saucepan, place closed mussels. Pour in around ½ cup water, just enough to reach the bottom of the pan by ¼ inch.
3. Set over high heat, covered. Bring to a boil and cook for 1 to 2 minutes, or until the shells have opened. Remove from the heat, switch to a tray, and leave to cool before you can handle it. Throw away those that haven't been opened. Place the cooked mussels in a medium bowl and remove the shells and cooking liquid.
4. Bring a 3-quart saucepan of water to a boil over high heat to cook the remaining seafood. Return the water to a boil after adding the salt. Pour the shrimp into the boiling water and cook for 2 minutes, or until the largest one is pink on the outside, opaque on the inside, and only cooked through. The water cannot come back to a boil until it is done. Scoop them out with a slotted spoon and place them in the same bowl as the mussels.
5. After the water returns to a rolling boil, add the squid and cook for around 1 minute, or until they become firm and the rings turn bright white. Scoop them out and toss them in with the shrimp and mussels in the tub.
6. When the water returns to a boil, cook the scallops for 1 to 2 minutes for bay scallops and 2 to 3 minutes for sea scallops, or until just cooked through and no longer translucent inside. Scoop them out and place them in the bowl as well (if using sea scallops, you may want to halve or quarter them first).
7. Add the lump crabmeat chunks to the seafood dish. Set the seafood aside on the counter as you make the dressing and other salad ingredients.

To make the dressing and salad

1. Combine the lime juice, fish sauce, sugar, chiles, and garlic in a medium-large mixing bowl. Stir to remove the sugar and thoroughly mix everything. Place aside.
Assemble the salad as follows:
2. Arrange the lettuce as a bed for the seafood on a big serving platter or individual serving plates.
3. Place the cooked seafood in the bowl with the lime-juice dressing. Add the shallots and gently toss everything together with your hands or a wooden spoon.
4. Mix in the scallions, cilantro, and mint until well combined. Using a slotted spoon, transfer the seafood to the platter or serving plates. Toss the cucumber and tomato in the remaining dressing in the tub, then scatter over the seafood.
5. Drizzle any leftover dressing from the bowl over the salad, paying particular attention to any lettuce that hasn't been covered by the seafood. Serve right away.

Serving Suggestion: Serve over a bed of rice; you can go for sticky rice, jasmine rice, or any other rice appropriate for Thai cuisine.

Variation Tip: Add coriander/oyster sauce during or after cooking for an additional flavorful punch.

Nutritional Information Per Serving:
Calories 403 | Fat 30g |Sodium 1387mg | Carbs 4g | Fiber 1g | Sugar 1g | Protein 28g

Sardines and Lemon grass

Prep Time: 15 minutes.
Serves: 4

Ingredients:
- 2 tablespoons Thai sweet chile sauce
- 1 tablespoon lime juice
- ½ teaspoon kosher salt
- 1 lemon grass, tough outer leaves discarded, and the inner core thinly sliced up
- 1 (3.75-ounce) can sardines, drained and cut up into 1-inch pieces
- 1 ½ cups lightly packed torn cilantro leaves
- ½ small red onion, sliced

Preparation:
1. Take a large-sized bowl whisk in the chile sauce, lime juice, and salt.
2. Mix well.
3. Add cilantro, lemon grass, sardines, and red onions.
4. Toss well.
5. Transfer to your serving platter and enjoy!

Serving Suggestion: Serve over a bed of rice; you can go for sticky rice, jasmine rice, or any other rice appropriate for Thai cuisine.

Variation Tip: Add oyster sauce during or after cooking for an additional flavorful punch.

Nutritional Information Per Serving:
Calories 227 | Fat 6g |Sodium 272mg | Carbs 29g | Fiber 3g | Sugar 4g | Protein 15g

Thai Prawn Salad (Pla Gung)

Prep Time: 10 minutes.
Cook Time: 5-6 minutes.
Serves: 4

Ingredients:
- 1 pound prawn tails
- 3 cups water
- 2 tablespoons lemon grass, coarsely chopped
- 1 tablespoon lime leaves, coarsely chopped
- 1 tablespoon coriander leaves, coarsely chopped
- 2 tablespoons lime juice

- 2 teaspoons palm sugar
- 1 teaspoon finely chopped garlic
- 1 teaspoon ginger, finely chopped
- ½ teaspoon ground black pepper
- ½ cup sliced green onions
- ½ cup mint leaves

Preparation:
1. Bring a pot of water to a boil, then add the lemon grass, lime leaves, and coriander. Cook for 5 minutes.
2. Cook for 1 minute after adding the prawns. Remove the item and clean it under cold water.
3. In a mixing bowl, combine lime juice, palm sugar, garlic, ginger, and black pepper. To dissolve the sugar, combine all of the ingredients.
4. Toss the prawns in the dressing to coat. Toss in the green onions and mint leaves.
5. Serve and enjoy!

Serving Suggestion: Serve over a bed of rice; you can go for sticky rice, jasmine rice, or any other rice appropriate for Thai cuisine.

Variation Tip: Add banana blossom during or after cooking for an additional flavorful punch.

Nutritional Information Per Serving:
Calories 251 | Fat 4g |Sodium 1196mg | Carbs 41g | Fiber 2g | Sugar 18g | Protein 15g

Thai Pumpkin Seafood Stew

Prep Time: 15 minutes.
Cook Time: 35 minutes.
Serves: 4

Ingredients:
- 1 ½ tablespoons fresh galangal, chopped
- 1 teaspoon lime zest
- 1 small kabocha squash, cut into chunks
- 32 medium-sized mussels, fresh
- 1 pound shrimp
- 16 Thai basil leaves
- 1 can coconut milk
- 1 tablespoon lemon grass, minced
- 4 garlic cloves, roughly chopped
- 32 medium clams, fresh
- 1 ½ pounds fresh salmon, cut into bite-size pieces
- 2 tablespoons coconut oil
- Pepper to taste

Preparation:
1. Add coconut milk, lemon grass, galangal, garlic, and lime zest in a small-sized saucepan, bring to a boil.
2. Let it simmer for 25 minutes.
3. Strain mixture through a fine sieve into the large soup pot and bring to a simmer.
4. Add oil to a pan and heat up; add kabocha squash.
5. Season with salt and pepper, sauté for 5 minutes.
6. Add mix to coconut mix.
7. Heat oil in a pan and add salmon and shrimp, season with salt and pepper, cook for 4 minutes.

8. Add mixture to coconut milk mix alongside clams and mussels.
9. Simmer for 8 minutes, garnish with basil and enjoy!

Serving Suggestion: Serve with some bread or fried rice.

Variation Tip: Add banana blossom/coriander/oyster sauce during or after cooking for an additional flavorful punch.

Nutritional Information Per Serving:
Calories 434 | Fat 18g |Sodium 741mg | Carbs 24g | Fiber 4 g | Sugar 6g | Protein 38g

Fine Thai Tilapia Dish

Prep Time: 15 minutes.
Cook Time: 20 minutes.
Serves: 4

Ingredients:
- ½ cup coconut milk
- 6 whole almonds
- 2 tablespoons chopped white onion
- 1 teaspoon ground ginger
- ½ teaspoon ground turmeric
- 1 teaspoon chopped fresh lemon grass
- ¼ teaspoon salt
- 4 ounces tilapia fillets
- Salt as needed
- Pepper as needed
- ½ teaspoon red pepper flakes

Preparation:
1. Take a food processor and add coconut milk, onion, almonds, ginger, turmeric, lemon grass, and ¼ teaspoon of salt.
2. Process well.
3. Take a large-sized skillet and place it over medium-high heat.
4. Season the fish fillets with salt and pepper on both sides.
5. Add them to the skillet skin side up.
6. Pour the pureed sauce over the fish.
7. Use a spatula to coat the fish evenly.
8. Sprinkle red pepper flakes.
9. Lower down the heat to medium and simmer for about 15 minutes.
10. Enjoy!

Serving Suggestion: Serve over a bed of rice; you can go for sticky rice, jasmine rice, or any other rice appropriate for Thai cuisine.

Variation Tip: Add banana blossom/basil/chili peppers/cilantro/coriander/oyster sauce during or after cooking for an additional flavorful punch.

Nutritional Information Per Serving:
Calories 211 | Fat 10g |Sodium 379mg | Carbs 3g | Fiber 1g | Sugar 0g | Protein 29g

Tamarind and Prawns (Goong Ma Kham)

Prep Time: 15 minutes + 30 minutes for marinating.
Cook Time: 4 minutes.
Serves: 4

Ingredients:
- Coriander leaves for garnish
- 21 ounces raw prawns, peeled and deveined
- 1 teaspoon freshly ground black pepper
- ¼ teaspoon crushed dried chili
- 2 tablespoons tamarind pulp
- 1 tablespoon light soy sauce
- ½ a teaspoon soft brown sugar
- Just a pinch salt
- 2 tablespoons vegetable oil

Preparation:
1. Take a bowl and add all of the ingredients except salt, oil, and prawn; mix them well.
2. Add prawns and cover them, leave them for about 30 minutes, making sure to turn them 2-3 minutes.
3. Season the prawns with salt.
4. Take a frying pan and place it over medium-high heat.
5. Add vegetable oil and allow it to heat up.
6. Add prawns and fry them for 2 minutes until both sides are dark brown.
7. Garnish them with some fresh coriander leaves and serve with some cucumber slices.
8. Enjoy!

Serving Suggestion: Serve over a bed of rice; you can go for sticky rice, jasmine rice, or any other rice appropriate for Thai cuisine.
Variation Tip: Add banana blossom/coriander/oyster sauce during or after cooking for an additional flavorful punch.
Nutritional Information Per Serving:
Calories 899 | Fat 55g |Sodium 252mg | Carbs 83g | Fiber 12g | Sugar 22g | Protein 20g

Thai Steamed Mussels

Prep Time: 15 minutes.
Cook Time: 10 minutes.
Serves: 4

Ingredients:
- 5 pounds fresh mussels, debearded and scrubbed
- ¼ cup fresh lime juice

- 1 can unsweetened coconut milk
- ¼ cup dry white wine
- 1 ½ tablespoons Thai red curry paste
- 1 ½ tablespoons garlic, minced
- 1 tablespoon Asian fish sauce
- 1 tablespoon white sugar
- 2 cups chopped fresh cilantro

Preparation:
1. Take a large-sized stock pot.
2. Add lime juice, coconut milk, wine, garlic, curry paste, fish sauce, and sugar.
3. Stir sugar and dissolve alongside the curry paste.
4. Bring it to a boil over high heat.
5. Boil for about 2 minutes.
6. Add mussels and cover, and cook for about 5-8 minutes.
7. Remove the heat and discard any unopened mussels.
8. Pour mussels and liquid into a serving dish.
9. Add cilantro, and enjoy!

Serving Suggestion: Serve over a bed of rice; you can go for sticky rice, jasmine rice, or any other rice appropriate for Thai cuisine.
Variation Tip: Add banana blossom/oyster sauce during or after cooking for an additional flavorful punch.
Nutritional Information Per Serving:
Calories 439 | Fat 26g |Sodium 1269mg | Carbs 16g | Fiber 1g | Sugar 3g | Protein 32g

Garlic and Pepper Shrimp

Prep Time: 25 minutes.
Cook Time: 10 minutes.
Serves: 4

Ingredients:
- 2 ½ tablespoons vegetable oil
- ¼ cup water
- 1 cup shredded cabbage
- 1 tablespoon garlic, minced
- 8 large-sized peeled and deveined shrimp
- 2 teaspoons crushed red pepper flakes
- 2 tablespoons sliced onion
- 1 tablespoon fresh cilantro, chopped
- 1 tablespoon soy sauce

Preparation:
1. Take a metal skillet and place it over high heat.
2. Add 1 tablespoon of oil and heat it up.
3. Add cabbage and 1 tablespoon of water to stir fry the cabbage for 30 seconds.
4. Remove your cabbage and place it on the serving platter.
5. Add 1 and a ½ tablespoon of oil to the skillet and place it over high heat again.
6. Add garlic and shrimp and cook until the shrimp turns pink.
7. Add your onion, pepper, cilantro, water, and soy sauce to the skillet.

8. Stir fry for about 10 seconds.

9. Pour the mix into the cabbage and serve!

Serving Suggestion: Serve over a bed of rice; you can go for sticky rice, jasmine rice, or any other rice appropriate for Thai cuisine.

Variation Tip: Add banana blossom during or after cooking for an additional flavorful punch.

Nutritional Information Per Serving:

Calories 182 | Fat 6g |Sodium 436mg | Carbs 24g | Fiber 1g | Sugar 0g | Protein 7g

Thai Fish and Vegetables Curry

Preparation Time: 10 minutes

Cooking Time: 15 minutes

Servings: 8

Ingredients:

• 3 pounds white fish, cut into chunks

• 4 tablespoons coconut oil

• 4 tablespoons finely minced ginger

• 2 cups coconut milk

• 2 tablespoons fish sauce

• 6 tablespoons red curry paste

• 1 onion, finely chopped

• 6 garlic cloves, finely minced

• 1 cup water

• 2 tablespoons brown sugar

• 8 cups chopped vegetables

Preparation:

1. Rub the red curry paste over the fish and allow it to sit to marinade.

2. At the same time, in a pot, add oil and heat. Add ginger, garlic, and onion in the pot and cook for about 5 minutes.

3. Add in fish sauce, water, coconut milk, and sugar in the pot and stir well.

4. Add the vegetables and stir. Bring all together to a boil.

5. Place the fish inside. Cover the lid and cook for about 5 minutes.

6. When cooked, remove from the pot and transfer to a serving plate.

7. Serve and enjoy!

Serving Suggestions: Garnish with cilantro before serving.

Variation Tip: Black pepper can also be used to enhance taste.

Nutritional Information per Serving:

Calories: 579 | Fat: 29.7g|Sat Fat: 21.1g|Carbs: 21g|Fiber: 5g|Sugar: 5g|Protein: 48.5g

Steamed Barramundi with Lime and Garlic

Preparation Time: 20 minutes

Cooking Time: 15 minutes

Servings: 2

Ingredients:

• 2 whole barramundi, guts and gills removed

• 10 lemongrass stalks, cut into chunks

• 2 cups fish stock

• 1 cup lime juice

• 4 garlic heads, chopped

• 30 sprigs cilantro, chopped

• 4 tablespoons palm sugar

• 12 tablespoons fish sauce

• Thai chilies, to taste

Preparation:

1. Fill the fish cavity with lemongrass and steam the fish over boiling water for about 15 minutes.

2. At the same time, in a pan boil fish stock and stir in sugar until completely dissolved. Then remove the stock from the pan and set aside for later use.

3. Add lime juice, cilantro, chilies, garlic, and fish sauce in the stock and mix well.

4. Transfer the fish in serving plates and drizzle with the fish stock mixture.

5. Serve with steamed rice. Enjoy!

Serving Suggestions: Garnish with chopped cilantro before serving.

Variation Tip: Chicken stock can be used instead of fish stock.

Nutritional Information per Serving:

Calories: 420 | Fat: 6.3g|Sat Fat: 0.5g|Carbs: 46.5g|Fiber: 1.7g|Sugar: 13.7g|Protein: 49.9g

King Prawn and Banana Salsa

Prep Time: 15 minutes.

Cook Time: 5 minutes.

Serves: 4

Ingredients:

• 2 bananas, peeled and sliced

• 2 cucumbers, peeled and diced

• ½ cup fresh mint leaves

- ½ cup fresh cilantro leaves
- 1 teaspoon fresh ginger root, finely chopped
- 1 fresh red chile pepper, sliced
- ¼ cup lime juice
- 1 tablespoon fish sauce
- 1 tablespoon brown sugar
- 1 and ½ pound tiger prawns, peeled and deveined

Preparation:
1. Take a large-sized bowl and add cucumbers, bananas, ginger, cilantro, red chile pepper, and mix everything well to prepare the salsa.
2. Take a small-sized bowl and add lime juice, fish sauce, brown sugar, and blend well until the mixture has fully dissolved.
3. Thoroughly mix up your salsa.
4. Take a large-sized saucepan and add a bit of lightly salted water; bring the water to a boil.
5. Add your prawns into the water and cook for 3 minutes.
6. Serve with your banana salsa!

Serving Suggestion: Serve over a bed of rice; you can go for sticky rice, jasmine rice, or any other rice appropriate for Thai cuisine.

Variation Tip: Add oyster sauce during or after cooking for an additional flavorful punch.

Nutritional Information Per Serving:
Calories 251 | Fat 4g |Sodium 1196mg | Carbs 35g | Fiber 7g | Sugar 18g | Protein 15g

Crispy Wonton-Wrapped Shrimp Rolls (Goong Gra Bok)

Prep Time: 5 minutes.
Cook Time: 5 to 10 minutes.
Serves: 4

Ingredients:
- 30 wonton wrappers
- 1 pound peeled, deveined, tail-on raw shrimp (about 30)
- Neutral oil, such as peanut or refined coconut oil, for frying
- Sweet chili sauce

Preparation:
1. Clean your work surface and place the wrappers.
2. Use your finger to straighten out each shrimp a bit and place it at the edge of one of the wrappers, leaving the tail off the wrapper.
3. Bring the remaining wrapper all the way over to cover the shrimp.
4. Then, use your thumbs to grab the edge on which the shrimp is lying and roll up to form a cylinder.
5. Use water at the tip of your finger to seal the wrapper.
6. Take a deep skillet over medium-high heat, heat 1 inch of oil to 375 degrees F.
7. Fry the rolls in batches.
8. Be careful not to overcrowd them, just until crisp and golden brown, 1 to 2 minutes.

9. Drain well on paper towels and serve with chili sauce for dipping.
10. Serve and enjoy!

Serving Suggestion: Serve them as a side with your main dishes, such as fried rice or curries.

Variation Tip: Add banana blossom/coriander/oyster sauce during or after cooking for an additional flavorful punch.

Nutritional Information Per Serving:
Calories 880 | Fat 27g |Sodium 1573mg | Carbs 114g | Fiber 4g | Sugar 2g | Protein 41g

Thai Shrimp Spring Rolls

Preparation Time: 30 minutes
Servings: 12
Ingredients:
- 24 small, round rice wrappers, dried
- 2 tablespoons rice vinegar
- 2 teaspoons brown sugar
- 2 cups cooked shrimp
- 1 cup fresh Thai basil, roughly chopped
- 2 tablespoons shredded carrot
- 4 tablespoons soy sauce
- 2 tablespoons fish sauce
- 3 cups rice noodles, cooked
- 4 cups bean sprouts
- 1 cup fresh coriander, roughly chopped
- 6 spring onions, chopped

Preparation:
1. In a cup, stir together the soy sauce, brown sugar, fish sauce, and rice vinegar. Mix well.
2. In a bowl, add shrimp, bean sprouts, basil, coriander, spring onions, carrots, and rice noodles and mix well.
3. Add the sauce mixture to the shrimp mixture and toss well to coat.
4. In a large bowl, pour warm water and submerge the rice wrappers in, about 30 seconds for each.
5. Remove the rice wrappers and then add shrimp mixture over. Evenly spread the mixture and then fold the edges of the rice wrappers.
6. Serve and enjoy!

Serving Suggestions: Serve with tamarind sauce.

Variation Tip: Use Roman coriander for an even better taste.

Nutritional Information per Serving:
Calories: 207 | Fat: 1.1g |Sat Fat: 0.2g |Carbs: 40.7g |Fiber: 2.4g |Sugar: 3.9g |Protein: 8.8g

Thai Fried Tilapia with Sweet and hot Chili Sauce

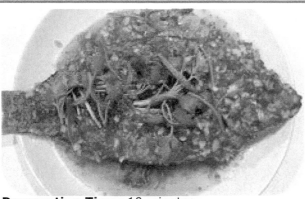

Preparation Time: 10 minutes
Cooking Time: 15 minutes
Servings: 2
Ingredients:
- 1 Nile Tilapia
- 1 Thai hot chili
- 1 tablespoon coconut sugar
- ½ cup vegetable oil
- ½ Thai long chili
- 2 garlic cloves
- 1 tablespoon fish sauce
- 1 tablespoon all-purpose flour

Preparation:
1. Rub the all-purpose flour over the fish. Then fry in the heated oil for 10 minutes, halfway through cooking flip once. Remove from heat and set aside for later use.
2. Then add hot chili, long chili, fish sauce, sugar, and garlic in the pan. Simmer for about 5 minutes to thicken the sauce.
3. Pour the thickened sauce over the fish. Serve and enjoy!

Serving Suggestions: Serve with steamed rice.
Variation Tip: You can also use honey in the sauce.
Nutritional Information per Serving:
Calories: 709 | Fat: 62.3g|Sat Fat: 12.2g|Carbs: 25.6g|Fiber: 0.4g|Sugar: 1.1g|Protein: 11.8g

Thai Coconut Fish

Preparation Time: 15 minutes
Cooking Time: 20 minutes
Servings: 2
Ingredients:
- 1 tablespoon butter

- 1 tablespoon red curry paste
- 1 cup coconut milk
- 1 teaspoon finely chopped gingerroot
- 2 tablespoons finely chopped shallots
- 1 tablespoon fish sauce
- 1 tablespoon lemongrass, chopped
- ½ pound cod fillets, cut into chunks
- ¼ cup sweetened flaked coconut, toasted
- ½ teaspoon freshly grated lime zest
- ½ tablespoons chopped cilantro

Preparation:
1. In a skillet, add butter and heat to melt. When heated, add shallots and cook for about 5 minutes.
2. Then add curry paste in the pan and stir for about 1 minute.
3. Add fish sauce, gingerroot, lemongrass, and coconut milk in the skillet and bring together to a boil. Let it simmer for about 6 minutes.
4. Add the cod and cook for about 7 minutes.
5. When the cod is cooked, remove from the skillet and transfer to a serving plate.
6. Mix together the sweetened coconut, cilantro, and lime zest in a bowl until well incorporated.
7. Drizzle the mixed sauce over the cod. Serve and enjoy!

Serving Suggestions: Serve with chili flakes on the top.
Variation Tip: Add chili sauce to enhance taste.
Nutritional Information per Serving:
Calories: 497 | Fat: 41g|Sat Fat: 32.7g|Carbs: 12.5g|Fiber: 3.6g|Sugar: 5g|Protein: 24.2g

Spicy Thai Garlic Shrimp

Preparation Time: 10 minutes
Cooking Time: 6 minutes
Servings: 2
Ingredients:
- ½ pound raw shrimp
- 1 tablespoon soy sauce
- 1 tablespoon honey
- ½ inch ginger, grated
- 2 tablespoons chopped onion
- 1 tablespoon sesame oil
- ½ tablespoons red pepper flakes
- 3 garlic cloves, minced

Preparation:
1. In a bowl, mix together the soy sauce, sesame oil, red pepper flakes, garlic, ginger, and honey.

2. Add the shrimp and mix to coat well.
3. At the same time, in a skillet, add oil and heat. Then add onion and sauté until just transparent.
4. Add marinated shrimp in the skillet and cook for around 6 minutes.
5. When cooked, remove from the skillet and transfer to a serving plate.
6. Serve and enjoy!

Serving Suggestions: Top with hot sauce before serving.
Variation Tip: Replace sesame oil with olive oil.
Nutritional Information per Serving:
Calories: 248 | Fat: 9g|Sat Fat: 1.6g|Carbs: 14.5g|Fiber: 0.8g|Sugar: 9.4g|Protein: 27g

Thai Stir-fried Shrimp with Basil

Preparation Time: 15 minutes
Cooking Time: 2 minutes
Servings: 2
Ingredients:
• 1½ Thai chilies, coarsely chopped
• 2 tablespoons sugar
• ½ teaspoon kosher salt
• ½ pound large shrimp, peeled and deveined
• 3 garlic cloves, smashed
• 1 tablespoon fish sauce
• 2 tablespoons vegetable oil
• 1 cup basil leaves
Preparation:
1. In a blender, blender together the sugar, chilies, fish sauce, garlic, salt, and 1 tablespoon of oil.
2. Remove from the blender and add the mixture in a bowl.
3. Then add shrimp and mix well to coat. Let it sit for 10 minutes to marinade.
4. Meanwhile, in a skillet, add the remaining oil and heat. Add shrimps and cook per side for 1 minute.
5. When cooked, remove the shrimp from the skillet and transfer into a serving bowl.
6. Add basil and mix together until the basil is wilted. Then transfer to the serving bowl.
7. Serve and enjoy!

Serving Suggestions: Serve with green chili sauce.
Variation Tip: Add a pinch of cayenne pepper to enhance taste.
Nutritional Information per Serving:
Calories: 956 | Fat: 27.5g|Sat Fat: 2.7g|Carbs: 145.4g|Fiber: 3g|Sugar: 20.6g|Protein: 36.2g

Authentic Thai Green Prawn Curry

Preparation Time: 7 minutes
Cooking Time: 10 minutes
Servings: 2
Ingredients:
• 2 tablespoons sunflower oil
• 4 garlic cloves, finely chopped
• 1 cup coconut milk
• ¼ pound prawns, cooked
• 2 teaspoons lemon juice
• 2 shallots, finely chopped
• 4 tablespoons Thai green curry paste
• ¾ cups sugar snap peas
• 2 teaspoons soy sauce
Preparation:
1. In a pan, add sunflower oil and heat. Then add shallots and garlic and fry for about 2 minutes.
2. Pour in coconut milk and green curry paste and cook for about 2 minutes.
3. Stir in sugar snap peas. Then add the lemon juice, soy sauce, and prawns and cook for around 5 minutes.
4. Remove from the pan and transfer to a serving plate.
5. Serve and enjoy!

Serving Suggestions: Serve with noodles.
Variation Tip: You can add chopped coriander to enhance taste.
Nutritional Information per Serving:
Calories: 841 | Fat: 68.5g|Sat Fat: 28.3g|Carbs: 37.7g|Fiber: 15.6g|Sugar: 12.2g|Protein: 23.2g

Thai Baked Salmon in Foil

Preparation Time: 5 minutes
Cooking Time: 20 minutes
Servings: 2
Ingredients:
• ¼ cup sweet chili sauce
• 1 garlic clove, minced
• ½ tablespoon freshly grated ginger

- 2 tablespoons peanuts, chopped
- 1 tablespoon reduced sodium soy sauce
- ½ tablespoon fish sauce
- 1 pound salmon
- 1 tablespoon fresh cilantro leaves

Preparation:
1. Before cooking, heat the oven to 375 degrees F. Prepare a baking sheet and line with a foil.
2. In a bowl, mix together fish sauce, chili sauce, ginger, garlic, and soy sauce.
3. Arrange the salmon on the foil and bake in the preheated oven for about 20 minutes.
4. Transfer to a serving plate and sprinkle the chopped peanuts on the top. Use cilantro leaves to garnish.
5. Serve and enjoy!

Serving Suggestions: Serve chopped basil leaves on the top.

Variation Tip: You can also add dried oregano.

Nutritional Information per Serving:
Calories: 425 | Fat: 18.6g|Sat Fat: 2.7g|Carbs: 15.9g|Fiber: 1.1g|Sugar: 12.7g|Protein: 47.3g

Fried Prawns with Basil

Preparation Time: 10 minutes
Cooking Time: 15 minutes
Servings: 4
Ingredients:
- 16 prawns, trimmed and deveined
- 8 garlic cloves, peeled and sliced
- 2 cups basil leaves
- 2 teaspoons dark soy sauce
- 2 teaspoons sesame oil
- 4 tablespoons vegetable oil
- 2 red chilies, sliced
- 2 tablespoons soy sauce
- 4 teaspoons sugar
- 4 teaspoons cornstarch
- ½ cup water

Preparation:
1. In a pan, add vegetable oil, chilies, and garlic.
2. Then add prawns and fry for 5 minutes.
3. Mix the prawns with dark soy sauce, soy sauce, sesame oil, sugar, and water.
4. Add cornstarch and basil leaves and stir occasionally.
5. When cooked, remove from the pan and transfer to a serving plate.

Serve and enjoy! **Serving Suggestions:** Serve with steamed rice.

Variation Tip: You can also use white pepper to enhance taste.

Nutritional Information per Serving:
Calories: 340 | Fat: 17.5g|Sat Fat: 3.5g|Carbs: 23.7g|Fiber: 0.5g|Sugar: 16.5g|Protein: 21.8g

Thai Baked Salmon with Lemongrass

Preparation Time: 15 minutes
Cooking Time: 35 minutes
Servings: 2
Ingredients:
- 1 tablespoon dark soy sauce
- ½ lemongrass stalk, finely sliced
- ½ teaspoon fresh ginger, grated
- 1 tablespoon honey
- 2 tablespoons rice vinegar
- 1 shallot, diced
- ½ pound salmon fillets

Preparation:
1. In a bowl, combine honey, dark soy sauce, and rice vinegar. Allow it to sit.
2. In another bowl, add ginger, shallot, and lemon grass. Set aside for later use.
3. Slit the salmon and coat with the ginger mixture.
4. Meanwhile, heat the oven to 275 degrees F and bake the salmon in the heated oven for about 35 minutes.
5. When cooked, remove from the oven and transfer to a serving plate.
6. Drizzle the soy sauce mixture on the top to serve.

Serving Suggestions: Serve with chopped coriander on the top.

Variation Tip: You can add lemon if you want.

Nutritional Information per Serving:
Calories: 251 | Fat: 7.1g|Sat Fat: 1g|Carbs: 22.9g|Fiber: 0.1g|Sugar: 20.8g|Protein: 22.7g

Thai Beef with Chilies and Basil (Phat Bai Horapha)

Prep Time: 15 minutes.
Cook Time: 15 minutes.
Serves: 3

Ingredients:
• 1 pound (450g) flank steak, skirt steak, hanger steak, or flap beef, thinly sliced
• 1 tablespoon (15ml) soy sauce,
• 5 teaspoons (25ml) Asian fish sauce
• 1 teaspoon (4g) granulated sugar
• 4 to 6 Thai bird's eye chilies, fresh red or green, divided
• 6 medium garlic cloves, divided
• 1 ½ tbsp (20g) palm sugar (see note)
• 1 small shallot, thinly sliced
• 4 makrut lime leaves, thinly sliced into hairs (central vein removed), plus more for garnish (see note)
• 2 tablespoons (30 mL) vegetable or canola oil, divided
• 2 cups packed Thai purple basil (approximately 2 oz; 55g)
• Red pepper flakes or Thai chili flakes, to taste(optional)
• ¼ cups fried shallots
• Kosher salt

Preparation:
1. In a mixing bowl, combine the meat, 1 teaspoon soy sauce, 2 teaspoons fish sauce, and white sugar. Toss all together and place in the refrigerator to marinate for at least 15 minutes and up to overnight.
2. Place half of the Thai chilies and garlic in a stone mortar with palm sugar. Using a pestle, grind until mostly smooth paste forms. Mash the remaining fish sauce and soy sauce in a mortar to make a sauce. Place aside. In a small bowl, finely slice the remaining garlic and chilies and mix with the shallot and lime leaves.
3. When you're ready to cook, heat 1 tablespoon oil in a wok over high heat until it begins to smoke. Cook, without moving the beef, until well seared, around 1 minute. Cook, stir, and constantly tossing until the beef is lightly cooked but still pink in spots, around 1 minute. Transfer to a big mixing bowl. Repeat with 1 tablespoon more oil and the remaining beef, moving beef to the same bowl each time. Wipe out the wok.
4. Reheat the wok over high heat and add the remaining beef and the sliced garlic/chili/makrut lime mixture. Cook, tossing, and stirring continuously, for 1 minute, or until the stir-fry is aromatic and the shallots are fully softened.
5. Cook, tossing, and stirring continuously until the sauce mixture is totally reduced in the wok. (The beef should appear moist, but there should be no liquid in the wok.) Toss in the basil right away to mix.
6. Season with salt and optional Thai chili or red pepper flakes to taste. Place on a serving platter. More makrut lime threads and fried shallots on top. Serve with rice right away.

Serving Suggestion: Serve over a bed of rice; you can go for sticky rice, jasmine rice, or any other rice appropriate for Thai cuisine.

Variation Tip: Add coriander/oyster sauce during or after cooking for an additional flavorful punch.

Nutritional Information Per Serving:
Calories 248 | Fat 17g |Sodium 339mg | Carbs 8g | Fiber 1g | Sugar 2g | Protein 16g

Fresh Thai Beef and Peanut Butter Dish

Prep Time: 10 minutes.
Cook Time: 10 minutes.
Serves: 4

Ingredients:
• 1 cup beef stock
• 4 tablespoons peanut butter
• ¼ teaspoon garlic powder
• ¼ teaspoon onion powder
• 1 tablespoon coconut amino
• 1 ½ teaspoons lemon pepper
• 1 pound beef steak, cut into strips
• Salt and pepper to taste
• 1 green bell pepper, seeded and chopped
• 3 green onions, chopped

Preparation:
1. Take a bowl and add peanut butter, beef stock, amino, lemon pepper, and stir.
2. Keep the mixture on the side.
3. Take a pan and place it over medium-high heat.
4. Add beef, season with salt, pepper, onion powder, and garlic powder.
5. Cook for 7 minutes.
6. Add green bell pepper, stir cook for 3 minutes.
7. Add peanut sauce and green onions.
8. Stir cook for 1 minute.
9. Divide between platters and serve.
10. Enjoy!

Serving Suggestion: Serve over a bed of rice; you can go for sticky rice, jasmine rice, or any other rice appropriate for Thai cuisine.

Variation Tip: Add oyster sauce during or after cooking for an additional flavorful punch.

Nutritional Information Per Serving:
Calories 219 | Fat 11g |Sodium 450mg | Carbs 14g | Fiber 4g | Sugar 5g | Protein 18g

Perfect Pork Dumplings (Khanom Jeeb)

Prep Time: 45 minutes.
Cook Time: 15 minutes.
Serves: 4

Ingredients:
For Garlic Oil
- 3 tablespoons vegetable oil
- 3 garlic cloves, minced

For Wonton
- 5 whole black peppercorns
- 2 garlic cloves, peeled, salt to taste
- 2 cilantro stems, chopped
- 5 ounces pork, ground
- 5 ounces minced shrimp
- 5 water chestnut, minced
- 1 tablespoon dark soy sauce
- 1 teaspoon white sugar
- 1 teaspoon fish sauce
- 1 tablespoon tapioca starch
- 1 teaspoon light soy sauce
- ½ tablespoon of salt
- 25 wonton wrappers (or as many as you need)

Sauce for Dipping
- 3 tablespoons rice vinegar
- 3 tablespoons light soy sauce
- 1 teaspoon white sugar
- 2 scallions, thinly sliced
- 1 bird's eye chili (or more as desired) (Optional)

Preparation:
1. In a small skillet over medium-low heat, heat the vegetable oil and add the minced garlic.
2. Cook until the garlic is golden brown for about 5 minutes. Remove the skillet from the heat.
3. Using a mortar and pestle, crush the peppercorns until they are powdery. Crush peeled garlic and a pinch of salt into a paste. Combine the cilantro stems with the paste.
4. In a big mixing bowl, add the paste, pork, shrimp, water chestnuts, dark soy sauce, 1 tablespoon white sugar, fish sauce, tapioca starch, light soy sauce, and ½ teaspoon salt. Mix well.
5. Fill each wonton wrapper with 1 to 2 teaspoons of the pork-shrimp mixture. Fold the wrapper over the filling to form a purse-like pouch, locking the edges together.
6. Fill a saucepan halfway with water to just below the bottom of a steamer insert. Get a pot of water to a boil. Cover and steam the wontons for about 10 minutes or until the filling is cooked through.
7. In a mixing bowl, combine rice vinegar, light soy sauce, 1 tablespoon white sugar, scallions, and bird's eye chili until well combined.
8. Serve Khanom Jeeb with dipping sauce and a drizzle of garlic oil on the side.

Serving Suggestion: Serve over a bed of rice; you can go for sticky rice, jasmine rice, or any other rice appropriate for Thai cuisine.
Variation Tip: Add oyster sauce during or after cooking for an additional flavorful punch.
Nutritional Information Per Serving:
Calories 374 | Fat 4g |Sodium 1620mg | Carbs 62g | Fiber 2g | Sugar 4g | Protein 21g

Thai Oven-baked Ribs

Preparation Time: 12 minutes + 24 hours for marinating
Cooking Time: 2 hours
Servings: 4
Ingredients:
- 4 tablespoons onion, minced
- 2 green chilies, minced
- 4 tablespoons fish sauce
- ½ cup brown sugar
- 4 tablespoons cornstarch
- 6 garlic cloves, minced
- ½ cup soy sauce
- 4 teaspoons rice vinegar
- 8 tablespoons maple syrup
- 4 pounds pork ribs

Preparation:
1. In a bowl, mix together the garlic, onion, chilies, rice vinegar, maple syrup, brown sugar, and soy sauce.
2. Add cornstarch in the mixture and whisk well. Allow it to sit for later use.
3. Meanwhile, place the ribs in a tray and drizzle over with the soy sauce mixture.
4. Marinate in the fridge for about 24 hours.
5. Before baking begins, heat the oven to 275 degrees F and bake for around 2 hours.
Serve and enjoy! **Serving Suggestions:** Serve with steamed rice.
Variation Tip: You can also use chili sauce to enhance taste.
Nutritional Information per Serving:
Calories: 1052 | Fat: 52.8g|Sat Fat: 20.2g|Carbs: 57.6g|Fiber: 0.7g|Sugar: 43.2g|Protein: 84.4g

Thai Waterfall Beef (Waterfall Dish)

Prep Time: 15 minutes.
Cook Time: 15 minutes.
Serves: 4

Ingredients:
• 1 to 2 steaks of sirloin (depending on the amount of meat you prefer)

Marinade:
• 2 tablespoons oyster sauce
• 2 tablespoons soy sauce
• 1 tablespoon lime juice (or lemon juice)
• 2 tablespoons brown sugar

Salad Ingredients:
• 6 cups mixed salad greens
• 1 cup sprouted bean
• 1 mint sprig (or basil, fresh, lightly chopped, or torn)
• 1 cup new coriander (fresh)
• 1 papaya cup (fresh, cubed, or cut into spears)
• 1 cup sliced tomatoes (cherry, left whole or sliced in half)

For Dressing:
• 1 to 2 tablespoons fish sauce (available at Asian food stores)
• 3 tablespoons lime juice (or lemon juice)
• 1 ½ tablespoons soy sauce
• 1 teaspoon cayenne pepper
• 1 teaspoon brown sugar
• 2 tablespoons rice (sticky variety, toasted and ground, OR 2 tbsp. ground peanuts)

Preparation:
1. In a cup or tub, combine the marinade ingredients, stirring to remove the sugar. Pour over the steak(s) and turn to coat. Place in the fridge to marinate.
2. Instead of peanuts, use sticky ground rice: In a dry frying pan over medium-high heat, heat 2 tablespoons uncooked sticky rice. Dry-fry the rice, constantly stirring, until it begins to pop and is lightly toasted. Enable the rice to cool slightly before grinding it with a coffee grinder or pounding it into a powder with a pestle and mortar.
3. In a cup or mixing bowl, whisk together all of the dressing ingredients until the sugar dissolves (adjust fish sauce according to your desired level of saltiness). Then, make your salad bowl with greens and other salad ingredients.
4. Grill the steak over a hot grill, rotating just once or twice to keep the juices in the steak (meat should still be pink in the center).
5. If broiling the steak in the oven, preheat the oven to broil. Place the steak on a broiling pan or a baking sheet lined with foil or parchment paper. Preheat the oven to the second-to-highest level. Broil the steak for 5 to 7 minutes per hand, or until it is well cooked on the outside but still pink on the inside.

6. Toss the salad with the dressing while the steak is cooking. Taste for salt, adding more fish sauce if it's not salty enough, or more lime juice if it's too salty.
7. When ready to serve, divide salad among serving plates or bowls. Thinly slice the steak and cover each section with a generous amount of sliced sirloin. Have fun!

Serving Suggestion: Serve over a bed of rice; you can go for sticky rice, jasmine rice, or any other rice appropriate for Thai cuisine.

Variation Tip: Add banana blossom/basil during or after cooking for an additional flavorful punch.

Nutritional Information Per Serving:
Calories 296 | Fat 14g |Sodium 778mg | Carbs 15g | Fiber 3g | Sugar 3g | Protein 29g

Spiced Beef and Broccoli

Prep Time: 10 minutes.
Cook Time: 15-20 minutes.
Serves: 4

Ingredients:
• ½ cup coconut milk
• 2 tablespoons coconut oil
• ¼ teaspoon garlic powder
• ¼ teaspoon onion powder
• ½ teaspoon coconut amino
• 1-pound beef steak, cut into strips
• Salt and pepper to taste
• 1 head broccoli, cut into florets
• ½ tablespoon Thai green curry paste
• 1 teaspoon ginger paste
• 1 tablespoon cilantro, chopped
• ½ tablespoon sesame seeds

Preparation:
1. Take a pan and place it over medium heat, add coconut oil and warm it.
2. Add beef, season with garlic powder, pepper, salt, ginger paste, and onion powder.
3. Cook for 4 minutes.
4. Mix in broccoli and stir fry for 5 minutes.
5. Pour coconut milk, coconut amino, Thai Curry paste and cook for 15 minutes.
6. Serve, sprinkle with cilantro, and sesame seeds.
7. Serve and enjoy!

Serving Suggestion: Serve over a bed of rice; you can go for sticky rice, jasmine rice, or any other rice appropriate for Thai cuisine.

Variation Tip: Add chili peppers/cilantro/coriander/oyster sauce during or after cooking for an additional flavorful punch.

Nutritional Information Per Serving:
Calories 116 | Fat 10g |Sodium 45mg | Carbs 5g | Fiber 3g | Sugar 1g | Protein 5g

Drunken Pork Stir Fry (Pad Kee Mao)

Prep Time: 20 minutes.
Cook Time: 20 minutes.
Serves: 4
Ingredients:
• 3 ½ ounces wide dried Thai-style rice noodles (such as Chan taboon Rice Noodles)
• ½ teaspoon olive oil
• 2 minced garlic cloves
• 1 teaspoon thick soy sauce
• 2 teaspoons white sugar
• ½ teaspoon olive oil
• 2 minced garlic cloves
• ½ pound thinly sliced pork (any cut)
• 1 serrano pepper, minced (or more as desired)
• 30 fresh basil leaves, chopped
• 1 teaspoon granulated sugar
• 1 teaspoon sea salt
• ½ cup steamed bean sprouts
Preparation:
1. Place the dry rice noodles in a cup, cover with hot water, and soak for 1 hour, or until white and softened. Drain and set aside the noodles.
2. In a wok or large skillet over low heat, heat 1 ½ teaspoon olive oil and cook and stir 2 minced garlic cloves until brown and beginning to crisp, 2 to 3 minutes.
3. Stir in the soaked noodles, ½ teaspoon thick soy sauce, and 2 teaspoons white sugar, and cook and stir for 3 minutes, or until the noodles have absorbed the soy sauce and turned brown. Take the noodles out of the skillet.
4. In the wok, heat the remaining 1 ½ teaspoons olive oil over low heat; add the remaining 2 minced garlic cloves and cook until brown and beginning to crisp, 2 to 3 minutes. Stir in the pork, serrano pepper, basil, ½ teaspoon thick soy sauce, 1 teaspoon sugar, and salt.
5. Cook and stir for 5 minutes, or until the pork is no longer pink and the edges of the meat begin to brown. Stir in the bean sprouts and return the noodles to the wok.
6. Cook and stir for another 5 minutes, or until thoroughly cooked.
Serving Suggestion: Serve over a bed of rice; you can go for sticky rice, jasmine rice, or any other rice appropriate for Thai cuisine.
Variation Tip: Add cilantro/coriander/oyster sauce during or after cooking for an additional flavorful punch.
Nutritional Information Per Serving:
Calories 405 | Fat 20g |Sodium 94mg | Carbs 33g | Fiber 3g | Sugar 24g | Protein 22g

Thai Pork Kabob (Pork Satay)

Prep Time: 45 minutes + 30 minutes for marinating.
Cook Time: 10 minutes.
Serves: 4
Ingredients:
• ¼ cup nutty peanut butter
• ¼ cup finely diced green onions
• 2 tablespoons soy sauce
• 2 teaspoons lemon juice
• 1 ½ tablespoons brown sugar
• 2 tablespoons minced garlic
• 1 teaspoon coriander powder
• ⅛ teaspoon cayenne pepper, ground
• 1 pound cubed pork tenderloin
• 1 (8 ounces) can drained water chestnuts
• 1 medium green bell pepper, diced into 2" bits
• 1 medium red bell pepper, peeled and cut into 2-inch pieces
• 1 small sweet onion, chopped
• skewers
Preparation:
1. In a medium mixing bowl, combine peanut butter, green onions, soy sauce, lemon juice, brown sugar, garlic, coriander, and cayenne pepper; stir in pork. Marinate in the refrigerator for at least 30 minutes, covered.
2. Preheat the grill to high. Alternately thread marinated pork, water chestnuts, green bell pepper, red bell pepper, and sweet onion onto skewers. Transfer the remaining marinade to a small saucepan, bring to a boil, and continue to cook for a few minutes.
3. Grates should be lightly oiled. Skewers should be cooked for 10 minutes or until finished to preference. Turn the skewers when grilling to ensure cooking and brush with the boiled marinade in the last few minutes.
Serving Suggestion: Serve over a bed of rice; you can go for sticky rice, jasmine rice, or any other rice appropriate for Thai cuisine or your desired dipping sauce.
Variation Tip: Add oyster sauce during or after cooking for an additional flavorful punch.
Nutritional Information Per Serving:
Calories 322 | Fat 16g |Sodium 1015mg | Carbs 23g | Fiber 3g | Sugar 17g | Protein 22g

Thai Fried Basil with Pork (Pad Krapow)

Prep Time: 15 minutes.
Cook Time: 10 minutes.
Serves: 4

Ingredients:
- 1-pound ground pork
- 3 tablespoons oil
- 5 minced garlic cloves
- 1 shallot
- 7 chopped green beans
- 2 bird's eye chili peppers
- 1 teaspoon brown sugar (white sugar is ok too)
- 1 tablespoon fish sauce
- 1 tablespoon light soy sauce
- 2 tablespoons dark soy sauce (for color)
- 2 tablespoons oyster sauce
- ⅓ cup chicken broth/water
- 1 cup Thai basil (leaves only)
- 1 egg (optional)

Preparation:
1. Cook your garlic and shallots in a big frying pan with vegetable oil over medium-high heat until fragrant and aromatic. After that, add your green beans and bird's eye chili. Cook for a few minutes at a time.
2. Increase the heat to high and add the ground pork, breaking it up to ensure even cooking. Cook until all of the pink is gone.
3. Combine fish sauce, brown sugar, light soy sauce, dark soy sauce, oyster sauce, and chicken broth in a mixing bowl. If the ground pork is cooked, apply this mixture to the pan and continue to cook until the sauce has reduced and the ground pork has caramelized.
4. Finally, add the Thai basil and cook until it begins to wilt. It's now time to eat.
5. Cook your egg in a frying pan over medium-low heat until it is cooked to your liking, then serve on top of the Pad Kra Pao.

Serving Suggestion: Serve over a bed of rice; you can go for sticky rice, jasmine rice, or any other rice appropriate for Thai cuisine. You may opt for Thai Fried Rice as well.

Variation Tip: Add cilantro/coriander/oyster sauce during or after cooking for an additional flavorful punch.

Nutritional Information Per Serving:
Calories 390 | Fat 29g |Sodium 754mg | Carbs 11g | Fiber 2g | Sugar 5g | Protein 21g

Thai Minced Pork Dish (Laab)

Prep Time: 10 minutes.
Cook Time: 10 minutes.
Serves: 4

Ingredients:
- 13 cups Canola oil
- 3 tablespoons mashed garlic
- 4 stemmed and minced Thai chiles
- 10 ounces ground pork
- 1 teaspoon crushed red pepper flakes
- 1 teaspoon Chinese five-spice powder
- 1 tablespoon freshly grated nutmeg
- 1 teaspoon kosher salt
- 14 teaspoon black pepper
- 14 teaspoon ground coriander
- 14 teaspoon ground cardamom
- 2 tablespoons minced mint, plus more for garnish
- 1 tablespoon minced scallions, plus more for garnish
- 1 tablespoon minced cilantro, plus more for garnish
- 2 tablespoons fish sauce
- thinly sliced kaffir lime leaves, lemon grass, scallions, shallots, cucumbers, and cherry tomatoes, for garnish

Preparation:
1. In a 12-inch skillet, heat the oil over medium heat. Cook, constantly stirring, until the garlic and chiles are fragrant, about 2 minutes.
2. Cook, constantly stirring until the pork is browned, about 2 minutes. Add the chili flakes, five-spice powder, nutmeg, salt, pepper, coriander, and cardamom.
3. Cook until the pork is cooked, about 4 minutes, after adding the mint, scallions, cilantro, and fish sauce.
4. Cover with scallions, cilantro, kaffir leaves, lemon grass, shallots, mint, cilantro, cucumbers, and tomatoes in a large serving dish. At room temperature, serve.

Serving Suggestion: Serve over a bed of rice; you can go for sticky rice, jasmine rice, or any other rice appropriate for Thai cuisine. You may opt for Thai Fried Rice as well.

Variation Tip: Add oyster sauce during or after cooking for an additional flavorful punch.

Nutritional Information Per Serving:
Calories 194 | Fat 14g |Sodium 472mg | Carbs 5g | Fiber 2g | Sugar 1g | Protein 12g

Authentic Chicken Fried Rice (Khao Pad)

Prep Time: 15 minutes.
Cook Time: 10-15 minutes.
Serves: 4

Ingredients:

To marinate the chicken
- ½ pound thinly sliced chicken
- 1 tablespoon tapioca flour
- 1 tablespoon Golden Mountain Sauce

To make the Chicken Fried Rice
- 2 eggs, lightly beaten with a pinch of salt
- 1 teaspoon finely chopped garlic
- 5 tablespoons vegetable oil
- 1 onion, chopped sliced coarsely
- ¼ cup fresh serrano or Thai chili peppers, sliced (seeds removed)
- 6 cups Jasmine rice, cooked (made the day before, left at room temp in rice cooker works best)
- 1 tablespoon Golden Mountain Sauce
- 2 tablespoons fish sauce
- 1 ½ tablespoons Roasted Chile Paste (namprik pao)
- ½ teaspoon salt
- 1 teaspoon lime juice
- 1 ½ tablespoons sugar
- ½ teaspoon Thai pepper powder
- ½ cup broccoli, cut into small floral florets
- 1 tomato, peeled and cut into wedges
- 2 tablespoons chopped green onion

Preparation:
1. Marinate the chicken in tapioca flour and Golden Mountain sauce for 10 minutes or so.
2. In a wok or skillet, heat 2 tablespoons of oil over medium heat.
3. Allow the eggs to cook before flipping them over and chopping them into smaller pieces with a spatula. Place the egg on a plate and set it aside.
4. Heat the remaining oil in the wok, then add the garlic and cook until golden brown. Stir-fry, the chicken for 3-4 minutes over high heat.
5. Combine the onion, chili pepper, and broccoli in a mixing bowl. Stir all together thoroughly. Pour the next 7 ingredients onto the cooked rice in a separate dish. Add all to the wok gently, stirring carefully to avoid crushing or breaking the rice.
6. Mix all thoroughly. Stir in the tomato, green onion, and egg for about a minute or two. Take the pan off the heat. Garnish with cucumber slices if desired. Have fun!

Serving Suggestion: You may serve with some chicken fry or your desired curry.

Variation Tip: Add banana blossom/oyster sauce during or after cooking for an additional flavorful punch.

Nutritional Information Per Serving:
Calories 618 | Fat 16g |Sodium 1005mg | Carbs 88g | Fiber 1g | Sugar 8g | Protein 27g

Thai Pineapple Chicken Curry

Prep Time: 15 minutes.
Cook Time: 35 minutes.
Serves: 4

Ingredients:
- 2 cups jasmine rice
- 1 quart water
- ¼ cup red curry paste
- 2 (13-ounce) cans coconut milk
- 2 skinless and boneless chicken breast halves, cut up into thin
- 3 tablespoons fish sauce
- ¼ cup white sugar
- 1 ½ cups sliced bamboo shoots
- ½ red bell pepper, julienned
- ½ green bell pepper, julienned
- ½ a small onion, chopped
- 1 cup pineapple chunks, drained up

Preparation:
1. Take a pot of water and bring water to a boil.
2. Add rice and lower down the heat to low.
3. Simmer for 25 minutes.
4. Take a bowl and add the curry paste and 1 can of coconut milk.
5. Transfer the mixture to a wok and add the rest of the coconut milk.
6. Add chicken, fish sauce, bamboo shoots, and sugar.
7. Bring it to a boil and cook further for 1 minute until the chicken juices run clear.
8. Take a bowl and mix red bell pepper, onion, and green bell pepper.
9. Add to the wok.
10. Cook for 10 minutes more until the chicken juices run clear.
11. Remove the heat and add pineapple.
12. Enjoy!

Serving Suggestion: Serve over a bed of rice; you can go for sticky rice, jasmine rice, or any other rice appropriate for Thai cuisine. You may opt for Thai Fried Rice as well.

Variation Tip: Add cilantro/coriander/oyster sauce during or after cooking for an additional flavorful punch.

Nutritional Information Per Serving:
Calories 349 | Fat 27g |Sodium 362mg | Carbs 19g | Fiber 5g | Sugar 6g | Protein 8g

Classic Thick Noodle with Chicken (Pad See Ew)

Prep Time: 15 minutes.
Cook Time: 10 minutes.
Serves: 4
Ingredients:
The Noodle
- 200g dried wide rice stick noodles (7 oz.) or 15 oz fresh wide flat rice noodles (450g) (Sen Yai)

Apple Sauce
- 2 tablespoons dark soy sauce
- 2 tablespoons oyster sauce
- 2 tablespoons soy sauce (all-purpose or light)
- 2 tablespoons white vinegar (plain white vinegar)
- 2 teaspoons sugar (any type)
- 2 tablespoons water

Stir-Fried
- 3 tablespoons divided peanut or vegetable oil
- 2 garlic cloves, very finely chopped 1
- 150g / 5oz. boneless, skinless chicken thighs (boneless, skinless), sliced
- 3 tablespoons divided peanut or vegetable oil
- 4 Chinese broccoli stems
- 1 egg

Preparation:
1. Trim the ends of the Chinese broccoli and cut it into 7.5cm/3-inch bits "fragments Separate the leaves from the roots. Thick stems should be cut in half vertically so that they are no wider than 0.8cm / 0.3 "dense.
2. Noodles - Cook and drain according to package instructions. Cook them only before using - if you leave cooked rice noodles lying around, they will break in the wok.
3. Sauce - Combine all of the ingredients in a mixing bowl and whisk until the sugar dissolves.

Cooking:
1. Heat 1 tablespoon oil in a big heavy-bottomed skillet or wok over high heat.
2. Cook for 15 seconds after adding the garlic. Cook until the chicken is mostly white and the color has changed from pink to white.
3. Cook until the chicken is almost finished, then add the Chinese broccoli stems.
4. Cook until the Chinese broccoli leaves are only wilted.
5. Push all to one side, smash an egg into the middle, and scramble. Place all on a plate (scrape wok clean).
6. Return the wok to the stove and heat 2 tablespoons of oil over high heat.
7. Toss in the noodles and sauce. Toss as little as possible to distribute the sauce and caramelize the edges of the noodles.
8. Return the chicken and vegetables to the pan and toss to combine. Serve right away!

Serving Suggestion: You may add some sweet chili sauce to go.
Variation Tip: Add banana blossom /oyster sauce during or after cooking for an additional flavorful punch.
Nutritional Information Per Serving:
Calories 529 | Fat 7g |Sodium 1386mg | Carbs 94g | Fiber 4g | Sugar 10g | Protein 20g

Fine Chicken Massaman Curry (Matasaman Curry)

Prep Time: 15 minutes.
Cook Time: 35 minutes.
Serves: 4
Ingredients:
- 2 tablespoons vegetable oil
- 3 tablespoons curry paste
- 1 sliced and minced ginger
- 1 ¼ pound skinless and boneless chicken breast meat, cubed
- 3 tablespoons brown sugar
- 3 tablespoons fish sauce
- 3 tablespoons tamarind paste
- ⅓ cup peanut butter
- 3 cups potatoes, peeled and cubed
- 1 can coconut milk
- 3 tablespoons fresh lime juice

Preparation:
1. Take a large-sized saucepan and place it over medium heat
2. Add oil and heat it up.
3. Add curry paste and minced ginger, stir fry for 2 minutes.
4. Stir in cubed up chicken and cook for about 3 minutes.
5. Stir in brown sugar, tamarind sauce, fish sauce, peanut butter, coconut milk, and potatoes.
6. Bring it to a boil.
7. Lower down the heat to medium-low and simmer for about 20 minutes until the chicken are no longer pink.
8. Add lime juice and cook for 5 minutes more.
9. Enjoy!

Serving Suggestion: Serve over a bed of rice; you can go for sticky rice, jasmine rice, or any other rice appropriate for Thai cuisine. You may opt for Thai Fried Rice as well.
Variation Tip: Add banana blossom during or after cooking for an additional flavorful punch.
Nutritional Information Per Serving:
Calories 682 | Fat 38g |Sodium 1297mg | Carbs 60g | Fiber 9g | Sugar 20g | Protein 33g

Perfect Thai Chicken Balls

Prep Time: 15 minutes.
Cook Time: 10 minutes.
Serves: 4

Ingredients:
- 2 pounds ground chicken
- 1 cup dry bread crumbs
- 4 green onion, sliced
- 1 tablespoon ground coriander seeds
- 1 cup fresh cilantro, chopped
- ¼ cup sweet chili sauce
- 2 tablespoons fresh lemon juice
- Oil for frying

Preparation:
1. Take a large-sized bowl and add chicken and bread crumbs.
2. Mix them well and season with some green onions, cilantro, ground coriander, lemon juice, and chili sauce.
3. Mix well.
4. Using damp hands, form evenly shaped balls using the mixture.
5. Take a large-sized skillet and place it over medium heat.
6. Add chicken balls and fry them until all sides are browned up.

Serving Suggestion: Serve with your desired dipping sauce, such as Sweet Thai Chili sauce or ketchup.

Variation Tip: Add banana blossom/basil/chili peppers/cilantro/coriander/oyster sauce during or after cooking for an additional flavorful punch.

Nutritional Information Per Serving:
Calories 466 | Fat 20g |Sodium 1272mg | Carbs 34g | Fiber 2g | Sugar 24g | Protein 42g

Thai Chicken Cashew Meal (Kai Med Ma Muang)

Prep Time: 15 minutes.
Cook Time: 15 minutes.
Serves: 4

Ingredients:
- 1 tablespoon canola oil
- ¾ cup cashew nuts
- 15 dried chiles
- 2 roughly chopped garlic cloves
- 1 ½ pounds chicken breast, cut up into 1-inch pieces
- 5 ounces quarter button mushrooms
- 3 tablespoons oyster sauce
- 1 tablespoon fish sauced
- 1 teaspoon sugar
- 1 jar (7 ounces) baby corn, drained and halved
- 1 bunch trimmed scallions cut in 1-inch pieces
- ½ cup cilantro leaves
- Cooked jasmine rice

Preparation:
1. Take a wok and place it over medium heat.
2. Add oil and heat it up.
3. Add cashews, chiles and cook for about 2 minutes.
4. Take a slotted spoon and transfer cashews to a bowl.
5. Add garlic and to the wok and cook for 1 minute.
6. Increase the heat to high and add chicken.
7. Cook for 3-5 minutes.
8. Add cashews, chiles, and mushrooms, fish sauce, oyster sauce, sugar, corn, scallion, and cook for 3 minutes until the chicken has been cooked.
9. Stir well.
10. Serve with some cilantro and over rice.

Serving Suggestion: Serve over a bed of rice; you can go for sticky rice, jasmine rice, or any other rice appropriate for Thai cuisine. You may opt for Thai Fried Rice as well.

Variation Tip: Add banana blossom /coriander/oyster sauce during or after cooking for an additional flavorful punch.

Nutritional Information Per Serving:
Calories 838 | Fat 58g |Sodium 6064mg | Carbs 23g | Fiber 2g | Sugar 7g | Protein 58g

Chicken Satay

Prep Time: 10 minutes.
Cook Time: 5 minutes.
Serves: 4

Ingredients:
- 1 pound ground chicken
- 4 tablespoons soy sauce
- 3 tablespoons peanut butter
- 2 spring onion
- ⅓ yellow bell pepper
- 1 tablespoon erythritol
- 1 tablespoon rice vinegar
- 2 teaspoons sesame oil
- 2 teaspoons chili paste
- 1 teaspoon minced garlic
- ⅓ teaspoon cayenne pepper
- ¼ teaspoon paprika
- juice of ½ lime

Preparation:
1. Heat up about 2 teaspoons of your sesame oil on medium high-heat pan.

2. Brown up your chicken and toss in all of the ingredients. Finely mix them and keep cooking.
3. Once cooked, toss in about 2 chopped up spring onions and ⅓ of your sliced yellow pepper.
4. Serve hot.
Serving Suggestion: Serve with your desired dipping sauce, such as Thai sweet chili sauce.
Variation Tip: Add cilantro/coriander/oyster sauce during or after cooking for an additional flavorful punch.
Nutritional Information Per Serving:
Calories 436 | Fat 15g |Sodium 1605mg | Carbs 5g | Fiber 1g | Sugar 2g | Protein 67g

Thai Chicken and Cabbage Lettuce Wraps

Preparation Time: 8 minutes
Cooking Time: 10 minutes
Servings: 2
Ingredients:
• 1 teaspoon olive oil
• 2 garlic cloves, minced
• ¼ teaspoon salt
• ½ carrot, shredded
• 1½ green onions, chopped
• ¼ pound chopped boneless, skinless chicken breasts
• ¼ cup yellow onion, chopped
• ¼ teaspoon black pepper
• ¼ cup cabbage, finely shredded
• ¼ cup sweet chili sauce
• ¼ teaspoon freshly grated ginger
• 2 tablespoons cilantro, chopped
• 1 head lettuce
• ½ tablespoon peanut butter
• 1 teaspoon low-sodium soy sauce
Preparation:
1. In a skillet, add olive oil and heat. When heated, add salt, pepper, garlic, yellow onion, and chicken and cook, tossing occasionally.
2. Add carrots, cabbage, and green onions in the skillet and cook for about 2 minutes.
3. In a bowl, combine together the peanut butter, ginger, soy sauce, and sweet chili sauce and then pour sauce in the skillet.
4. Add cilantro and stir to coat well.
5. When cooked, remove from the heat and transfer to a serving plate lined with lettuce cups.
6. Serve and enjoy!
Serving Suggestions: Serve with chopped mint leaves on the top.
Variation Tip: Add red pepper flakes to enhance taste.
Nutritional Information per Serving:
Calories: 268 | Fat: 9g|Sat Fat: 1.9g|Carbs: 25.6g|Fiber: 3.4g|Sugar: 16.8g|Protein: 19.7g

Awesome Ginger Chicken with Jasmine Rice

Prep Time: 35 minutes.
Cook Time: 40 minutes.
Serves: 4
Ingredients:
• 1 cup jasmine rice, uncooked
• ¼ teaspoon turmeric powder
• 1 ¼ pounds skinless, boneless chicken breast halves, cut into thin strips
• 3 tablespoons canola oil
• 1 small eggplant, quartered lengthwise, then crosswise into ½-inch-thick slices
• 1 large red bell pepper, sliced into 2-inch strips
• 1 large onion, cut in half and thinly sliced into ½-inch slices
• ¼ cup Swanson® Thai Ginger Flavor Infused Broth
• 2 minced garlic cloves
• ¾ cup coconut milk (unsweetened)
• 2 seeded and chopped jalapeno peppers
• 1 cup cilantro leaves, fresh
Preparation:
1. Cook the rice according to package directions, adding the turmeric to the cooking water halfway through.
2. In a 12-inch skillet, heat 1 tablespoon oil over medium-high heat. Cook, frequently stirring until the chicken is browned. Take the chicken out of the skillet.
3. In the skillet, heat the remaining oil. Cook, occasionally stirring, for 5 minutes, or until the eggplant, red pepper, and onion are tender-crisp. Cook and stir for 1 minute after adding the garlic. Bring the broth to a boil, then remove it from the heat. Turn the heat down to medium. Cook, occasionally stirring, for 8 minutes.
4. In a blender, combine the coconut milk, jalapeno peppers, and cilantro. Blend until the mixture is smooth, then cover and set aside.
5. In the skillet, stir the coconut milk mixture. Put the chicken back in the skillet. Cook until the chicken is thoroughly cooked. Serve the chicken and rice mixture together.
Serving Suggestion: You may consider some dipping sauce such as soy sauce or Chili Sauce.
Variation Tip: Add coriander/oyster sauce during or after cooking for an additional flavorful punch.
Nutritional Information Per Serving:
Calories 760 | Fat 35g |Sodium 2005mg | Carbs 62g | Fiber 1g | Sugar 18g | Protein 47g

Creamy Chicken Coconut Dish (Chicken Khao Soi)

Prep Time: 15 minutes.
Cook Time: 25-30 minutes.
Serves: 4
Ingredients:
- 1 box (6 oz.) chow Mein stir-fry noodles
- 1 can (13.5 oz.) coconut milk
- ¾ cup drained jarred roasted red peppers
- 1 ½ tablespoons canola oil
- 3 minced garlic cloves
- 2 shallots, sliced
- 3 tablespoons red curry paste
- 1 ½ tablespoons finely grated ginger
- 2 tablespoons chili powder
- 3 cups chicken broth
- 2 pounds skinless, boneless chicken thighs
- 1 teaspoon fish sauce
- 1 tablespoon low-sodium soy sauce
- 2 tablespoons brown sugar
- 2 tablespoons freshly squeezed lime juice
Garnish
- ½ tiny thinly sliced red onion
- ½ cup bean sprout
- ½ cup cilantro leaf
- 1 lime, cut into wedges
Preparation:
1. Cook the noodles according to the package directions; set aside.
2. Blend the coconut milk and red bell peppers until smooth; set aside.
3. In a big stockpot or Dutch oven, heat the canola oil over medium heat. Cook, frequently stirring, until the garlic and shallot are tender, around 3-4 minutes.
4. Stir in the red curry paste, ginger, and chili powder for around 1 minute, or until fragrant.
5. Scrape any browned bits from the bottom of the pot and stir in the chicken stock and coconut milk mixture.
6. Combine the chicken, fish sauce, soy sauce, and brown sugar in a mixing bowl. Bring to a boil; reduce heat and cook, stirring periodically, for 15-20 minutes, or until slightly reduced and chicken is tender.
7. Return the chicken to the pot and shred with two forks; stir in lime juice.
8. Serve immediately with noodles and, if desired, garnished with red onion, bean sprouts, cilantro, and lime.
Serving Suggestion: Serve over a bed of rice; you can go for sticky rice, jasmine rice, or any other rice appropriate for Thai cuisine. You may opt for Thai Fried Rice as well.

Variation Tip: Add cilantro/coriander/oyster sauce during or after cooking for an additional flavorful punch.
Nutritional Information Per Serving:
Calories 303 | Fat 21g |Sodium 662mg | Carbs 16g | Fiber 1g | Sugar 7g | Protein 15g

Thai Chicken Skewers with Peanut Sauce

Preparation Time: 8 minutes
Cooking Time: 15 minutes
Servings: 7
Ingredients:
- 1 cup coconut milk
- ½ pound chicken thighs, chopped
- ½ teaspoon sugar
- ¼ cup peanut butter
- 1 teaspoon dark soy sauce
- 1 tablespoon cider vinegar
- ½ tablespoon curry powder
- 1 teaspoon red curry paste
- 2 tablespoons white sugar
- ½ cup water
- Salt, to taste
Preparation:
1. In a bowl, mix the chicken and ¼ cup coconut milk.
2. On each skewer, thread 4 to 5 chicken pieces. Set aside for later use.
3. In a pan, add cooking oil and heat. When heated, cook the chicken skewers for about 3 minutes per side.
4. At same time, mix together curry powder, peanut butter, sugar, white sugar, soy sauce, red curry paste, cider vinegar, water, and sugar in a bowl.
5. Then in a pan, combine the peanut butter mixture and the remaining coconut milk and cook over medium-low heat for about 5 minutes.
6. When cooked, pour the prepared sauce over the chicken skewers.
7. Serve and enjoy!
Serving Suggestions: Serve with chopped peanuts on the top.
Variation Tip: Almond milk can be used instead of coconut milk.
Nutritional Information per Serving:
Calories: 218 | Fat: 15.5g|Sat Fat: 9g|Carbs: 8.7g|Fiber: 1.5g|Sugar: 5.8g|Protein: 12.7g

Tasty Thai Garlic Chicken Breast

Prep Time: 10 minutes.
Cook Time: 25-30 minutes.
Serves: 4

Ingredients:
- 1 pound chicken breast tenders
- Cooking spray as needed
- ¼ cup garlic chili sauce
- 2 tablespoons honey
- 1 teaspoon salt
- 1 teaspoon pepper
- 2 cups asparagus spears, chopped
- 1 cup onion, sliced
- 1 tablespoon olive oil
- Cooked rice for serving

Preparation:
1. Preheat your oven to 375 degrees F.
2. Spray 8x8 baking dish with cooking spray.
3. Place chicken in a single layer in a baking dish, season with salt and pepper.
4. Take a bowl and add garlic chili sauce, honey, and mix well.
5. Pour sauce mixture over chicken, add asparagus and onion.
6. Drizzle olive oil.
7. Bake for 25-30 minutes.
8. Remove from oven and let it rest.
9. Enjoy!

Serving Suggestion: Serve over a bed of rice; you can go for sticky rice, jasmine rice, or any other rice appropriate for Thai cuisine. You may opt for Thai Fried Rice as well.

Variation Tip: Add coriander/oyster sauce during or after cooking for an additional flavorful punch.

Nutritional Information Per Serving:
Calories 235 | Fat 17g |Sodium 230mg | Carbs 1g | Fiber 0g | Sugar 0g | Protein 18g

Lovely Fried Chicken (Gai Tod)

Prep Time: 15 minutes.
Cook Time: 10-15 minutes.
Serves: 4

Ingredients:
- 1 pound chicken wings
- 1 tablespoon coriander seeds, dried
- 1 tablespoon white pepper (substitute black pepper if white pepper is unavailable)
- 4 cloves garlic
- 3 tablespoons Thai Soy Sauce (Golden Mountain)
- 1 tablespoon dark Thai soy sauce
- 14 teaspoons salt
- 1 cup water
- flour made from rice
- 4 shallots, thinly sliced, deep-fried

Preparation:
1. Using a mortar and pestle, pound the dry ingredients (dried coriander seeds, black pepper, white pepper, and garlic cloves) into a paste. A food processor may also be used to make a fast 2-minute marinade.
2. Mix in the wet ingredients (Thai soy sauce, dark soy sauce, salt, and water). Pour marinade sauce over chicken wings and set aside (covered) for several hours, preferably overnight.
3. Garnish the chicken with the deep-fried shallots. Remove the chicken wings from the marinade and dredge in rice flour before frying for 4-6 minutes, or until brown and crispy.
4. For dipping, serve with sticky rice and sweet Thai chili sauce.

Serving Suggestion: Serve over a bed of rice; you can go for sticky rice, jasmine rice, or any other rice appropriate for Thai cuisine. You may opt for Thai Fried Rice as well. You may go for a nice dipping sauce such as Sweet Chili sauce as well.

Variation Tip: Add banana blossom/basil during or after cooking for an additional flavorful punch.

Nutritional Information Per Serving:
Calories 554 | Fat 49g |Sodium 538mg | Carbs 2g | Fiber 0g | Sugar 1g | Protein 25g

Exquisite and Exciting Thai Curries

Thai Monkfish Curry

Prep Time: 20 minutes.
Cook Time: 20 minutes.
Serves: 4
Ingredients:
- 1 teaspoon peanut oil
- 12 finely chopped sweet onion
- 1 chopped red bell pepper
- 3 tablespoons red Thai curry paste
- 1 can (14 oz.) coconut milk
- 12 ounces monkfish, cubed
- 1 teaspoon fish sauce
- 2 teaspoons lime juice
- 2 tablespoons cilantro, chopped
Preparation:
1. In a large sauce pan over medium heat, heat the peanut oil. Cook until the onion is softened and translucent, 3 to 5 minutes. Cook for 3 to 5 minutes more, or until red bell pepper is softened. Cook for 1 minute after adding the curry paste. Pour in the coconut milk and bring to a gentle simmer.
2. When the coconut milk starts to boil, add the cubed monkfish and cook for 7 to 10 minutes, or until the fish is firm and the middle is no longer opaque. Until serving, combine the fish sauce, lime juice, and cilantro.
Serving Suggestion: Serve over a bed of rice; you can go for sticky rice, jasmine rice, or any other rice appropriate for Thai cuisine. You may opt for Thai Fried Rice as well.
Variation Tip: Add chili peppers/cilantro/coriander/oyster sauce during or after cooking for an additional flavorful punch.
Nutritional Information Per Serving:
Calories 593 | Fat 22g |Sodium 2010mg | Carbs 29g | Fiber 4g | Sugar 4g | Protein 68g

Traditional Coconut Shrimp Curry

Prep Time: 15 minutes.
Cook Time: 120 minutes.
Serves: 4
Ingredients:
- 1 pound shrimp, with shells
- 3 ¾ cups light coconut milk
- 1 ¾ cups water
- ½ cup Thai red curry sauce
- 2 ½ teaspoons lemon garlic seasoning
- ¼ cup cilantro
Preparation:
1. Add coconut milk, red curry sauce, water, lemon garlic seasoning, and cilantro to your Slow Cooker.
2. Give it a nice stir.
3. Cook on HIGH for 2 hours.
4. Add shrimp and cook for another 15-30 minutes.
5. Garnish with some cilantro and serve!
Serving Suggestion: Serve over a bed of rice; you can go for sticky rice, jasmine rice, or any other rice appropriate for Thai cuisine. You may opt for Thai Fried Rice as well.
Variation Tip: Add banana blossom/basil/chili peppers during or after cooking for an additional flavorful punch.
Nutritional Information Per Serving:
Calories 239 | Fat 17g |Sodium 653mg | Carbs 7g | Fiber 1g | Sugar 2g | Protein 17g

Authentic Green Curry Prawn

Prep Time: 25 minutes.
Cook Time: 15 minutes.
Serves: 4
Ingredients:
- ½ teaspoon cumin powder
- 1 ½ teaspoons coriander powder
- 1 tablespoon fresh ginger root, minced
- 4 tablespoons minced garlic
- ⅓ cup chopped fresh cilantro
- 2 green chili peppers, chopped
- 3 stalks lemon grass, minced
- 1 lime, zested
- 2 limes, juiced
- 2 teaspoons corn oil
- ¼ cup corn oil
- ½ pound fresh green beans, trimmed
- 1 (7 ounces) can drained baby corn
- 1 teaspoon soy sauce
- 1 can (14 oz.) coconut milk
- ¾ pound medium peeled and deveined shrimp (30-40 per pound)
Preparation:

1. In a food processor, combine cumin, coriander, ginger, garlic, green chili peppers, lemon grass, cilantro, lime juice, lime zest, and 2 tablespoons corn oil.
2. To make a smooth, dense paste, combine all of the ingredients in a food processor. Place aside.
3. In a wide skillet over medium-high heat, heat ¼ cup corn oil. Green beans and baby corn should be cooked and stirred for about 30 seconds.
4. Bring to a boil with the paste, soy sauce, and coconut milk.
5. Reduce the heat to medium and cook for 5 to 7 minutes before adding the shrimp. 3 to 5 minutes, or until the shrimp are bright pink on the outside, and the meat is no longer translucent in the middle.
6. If the sauce becomes too thick, add a splash of water.

Serving Suggestion: Serve over a bed of rice; you can go for sticky rice, jasmine rice, or any other rice appropriate for Thai cuisine. You may opt for Thai Fried Rice as well.

Variation Tip: Add banana blossom during or after cooking for an additional flavorful punch.

Nutritional Information Per Serving:
Calories 400 | Fat 31g |Sodium 727mg | Carbs 13g | Fiber 2g | Sugar 3g | Protein 21g

Thai Potato Yellow Curry

Prep Time: 15 minutes.
Cook Time: 20 to 30 minutes.
Serves: 4
Ingredients:
• 1 tablespoon olive oil
• ½ yellow onion, sliced
• 1 pound boneless skinless chicken breasts, diced
• 3 tablespoons yellow curry paste
• 10 baby golden Yukon potatoes, peeled and diced
• 1 14-ounce can coconut cream (similar to coconut milk, but much more decadent)
• ½ cup water
• 2 tablespoons fish sauce (optional)
• ½–¼ tablespoon brown sugar (optional)
Preparation:
1. In a large pot, heat the oil over medium-low heat. Sauté the onions for a few minutes, or until they are fragrant and softened. Cook for 3-5 minutes after adding the chicken and curry paste. Stir in the potatoes to coat with the curry paste.
2. Add the coconut cream and ½ cup of water to the pot and lower down heat, simmer for 20-30 minutes, Until the chicken and potatoes are completely cooked, adding more water as required to achieve the desired sauce consistency.
3. To kick it up a notch, add the fish sauce and brown sugar. Seriously, it's fantastic. Serve with rice.
Serving Suggestion: Serve over a bed of rice; you can go for sticky rice, jasmine rice, or any other rice

appropriate for Thai cuisine. You may opt for Thai Fried Rice as well.

Variation Tip: Add coriander/oyster sauce during or after cooking for an additional flavorful punch.

Nutritional Information Per Serving:
Calories 286 | Fat 11g |Sodium 161mg | Carbs 35g | Fiber 13g | Sugar 18g | Protein 17g

Classic Thai Pineapple Chicken Curry

Preparation Time: 10 minutes
Cooking Time: 50 minutes
Servings: 3
Ingredients:
• 1 cup cooked jasmine rice
• 2 tablespoons red curry paste
• 1 chicken breast, cut into strips
• 2 tablespoons white sugar
• ¼ red bell pepper, julienned
• ¼ small onion, chopped
• 2 cups water
• ¾ cup coconut milk
• 1½ tablespoons fish sauce
• ½ cup bamboo shoots, drained
• ¼ green bell pepper, julienned
• ½ cup pineapple chunks, drained
Preparation:
1. In a pot, add water and rice and cook for about 25 minutes.
2. Stir in coconut milk, fish sauce, chicken, bamboo shoots, sugar, and red curry paste and cook for 15 minutes.
3. Add green bell pepper, onion, and red bell pepper in the pot and cook for about 10 minutes.
4. Take out and add pineapple chunks and stir well.
5. Serve and enjoy!
Serving Suggestions: Serve with chopped minty leaves on top.
Variation Tip: You can also use oregano to enhance taste.
Nutritional Information per Serving:
Calories: 505 | Fat: 18.3g|Sat Fat: 13.7g|Carbs: 70.6g|Fiber: 5.8g|Sugar: 16.4g|Protein: 15.4g

Pork Red Curry with Squash (Gaeng Daeng Sai Fak Thong Lae Moo)

Prep Time: 15 minutes.
Cook Time: 25 minutes.
Serves: 2
Ingredients:
• 1 tablespoon vegetable oil
• 1 tablespoon red curry paste (or to taste)
• 12 pounds thinly sliced pork loin
• 1 can (14 oz.) coconut milk
• 2 ¼ cups butternut squash, peeled and cubed
• 2 ¼ cups coarsely chopped cabbage
• 1 tablespoon fish sauce (or more to taste)
• 1 tablespoon white sugar (or more to taste)
Preparation:
1. In a medium pot, heat the oil over medium heat. Stir in the curry paste for 2 to 3 minutes, or until fragrant. Pork should be included.
2. Stir fry for 3 to 5 minutes more, until cooked through and coated in curry paste. Bring the coconut milk to a gentle boil. Squash should be included.
3. Reduce heat to low and cook until squash is just tender, 7 to 10 minutes.
4. Cook for 5 minutes more after adding the cabbage. Season with fish sauce and sugar to taste.
Serving Suggestion: Serve over a bed of rice; you can go for sticky rice, jasmine rice, or any other rice appropriate for Thai cuisine. You may opt for Thai Fried Rice as well.
Variation Tip: Add banana blossom/ coriander/oyster sauce during or after cooking for an additional flavorful punch.
Nutritional Information Per Serving:
Calories 536 | Fat 41g |Sodium 1251mg | Carbs 17g | Fiber 5g | Sugar 4g | Protein 31g

Thai Broccoli and Chickpea Curry

Prep Time: 15 minutes.
Cook Time: 15 minutes.
Serves: 4
Ingredients:
• 2 tablespoons cooking oil
• 2 garlic cloves, minced
• ¼ cup Thai red curry paste
• 2 heads broccoli, cut into florets
• 15 ounces/425 grams coconut milk
• 14 ounces/396 grams chickpeas, drained and rinsed
• 1 tablespoon cornstarch, dissolved in ¼ cup cold water
Preparation:
1. Build a campfire by arranging a bed of coal and letting the fire burn until coals are red hot, 12 coals on bottom.
2. Place Dutch Oven over hot coal, add garlic, and cook for 3 minutes.
3. Stir in curry paste, cook for 1 minute.
4. Add broccoli and cook for 2-3 minutes.
5. Add coconut milk, cook for 3 minutes.
6. Add chickpeas, bring back to boil.
7. Stir in cornstarch mixture and cook well for 2 minutes more.
8. Once the sauce is thick, serve and enjoy!
For stovetop cooking, the required temperature (approximately) is 325 degrees F /160 degrees C for a 10-inch Dutch oven.
Serving Suggestion: Serve over a bed of rice; you can go for sticky rice, jasmine rice, or any other rice appropriate for Thai cuisine. You may opt for Thai Fried Rice as well.
Variation Tip: Add banana blossom/basil/chili peppers during or after cooking for an additional flavorful punch.
Nutritional Information Per Serving:
Calories 321 | Fat 20g |Sodium 179mg | Carbs 29g | Fiber 5g | Sugar 7g | Protein 10g

Authentic Green Curry (Gaeng Keow Wan Gai)

Prep Time: 15 minutes.
Cook Time: 40-50 minutes.
Serves: 4
Ingredients:
• 3 pounds frying boneless skinless chicken cut into tiny chunks
• 4 cups coconut milk
• 2 teaspoons fish sauce
• 3 teaspoons Laos powder
• 3 tablespoons green curry paste (see my recipe)
• ½ cup sweet basil leaves, new
• 8 lime leaves, young and new
• ½ cup fresh green peas

• 7 serrano peppers
Preparation:
1. In a wok or big frying pan, combine the chicken, 2 cups of coconut milk, fish sauce, and Laos powder, and bring to a boil, cooking until the chicken is cooked and tender.
2. With a slotted spoon, remove your chicken from the pan, leaving everything else behind, and place it on a plate to set aside.
3. Allow the milk to boil until it is very thick and "oily."
4. After that, apply your curry paste to the pan.
5. Allow for 3 minutes of cooking time, or until all is smooth and even.
6. Return the chicken to the pan, pour in the remaining coconut milk, and bring the whole mixture to a boil.
7. Reduce the heat to low and leave it to cook for about 10 minutes.
8. Finally, add your basil and citrus leaves, peas, and serrano peppers, and bring to a boil for 5 minutes.
9. Serve right away.
Serving Suggestion: Serve over a bed of rice; you can go for sticky rice, jasmine rice, or any other rice appropriate for Thai cuisine. You may opt for Thai Fried Rice as well.
Variation Tip: Add chili peppers/cilantro/coriander/oyster sauce during or after cooking for an additional flavorful punch.
Nutritional Information Per Serving:
Calories 3225 | Fat 26g |Sodium 722mg | Carbs 10g | Fiber 1g | Sugar 1g | Protein 16g

Curried Coconut Chicken

Prep Time: 15 minutes.
Cook Time: 50 minutes.
Serves: 4
Ingredients:
• 2 pounds chicken breast, cut up into ½ inch chunks
• 1 teaspoon pepper and salt, each
• 1 ½ tablespoons vegetable oil
• 2 tablespoons curry powder
• ½ onion, thinly sliced
• 2 crushed garlic cloves
• 1 (14-ounce) can coconut milk
• 1 (14.5-ounce) can stewed diced tomatoes
• 1 (8-ounce) can tomato sauce
• 3 tablespoons sugar
Preparation:
1. Season your chicken with pepper and salt.
2. Take a large-sized skillet and heat up some oil over medium-high heat.
3. Add the curry powder and stir cook for 2 minutes.
4. Stir in your onions and garlic and cook for another minute.
5. Add your chicken, making sure to toss it well, and coat it up with the curry oil.

6. Lower down the heat to medium and cook the chicken for about 10 minutes.
7. Pour the coconut milk, tomato sauce, tomatoes, sugar into your pan and stir everything to combine it well.
8. Cover it up and simmer it for about 40 minutes.
9. Serve!
Serving Suggestion: Serve over a bed of rice; you can go for sticky rice, jasmine rice, or any other rice appropriate for Thai cuisine. You may opt for Thai Fried Rice as well.
Variation Tip: Add banana blossom/cilantro/coriander/oyster sauce during or after cooking for an additional flavorful punch.
Nutritional Information Per Serving:
Calories 300 | Fat 24g |Sodium 342mg | Carbs 8g | Fiber 2g | Sugar 2g | Protein 14g

Authentic Lentil Chickpea Yellow Curry

Preparation Time: 7 minutes
Cooking Time: 23 minutes
Servings: 4
Ingredients:
• ¼ cup lentils
• 1 cup chickpeas
• 1 ½ tablespoons yellow curry paste
• 1 cup coconut milk
• 3 garlic cloves, peeled and chopped
• ½ onion, chopped
• Salt, to taste
Preparation:
1. In a large skillet, add onion and garlic and fry for about 3 minutes.
2. Add coconut milk, lentils, and yellow curry paste and cook for about 15 minutes.
3. Add the chickpeas and cook for about 5 minutes, stirring well.
4. Remove and serve hot. Enjoy!
Serving Suggestions: Squeeze lemon in the curry before serving.
Variation Tip: You can also use cashew butter to fry onion and garlic.
Nutritional Information per Serving:
Calories: 405 | Fat: 20.9g|Sat Fat: 13g|Carbs: 44g|Fiber: 15.2g|Sugar: 8.2g|Protein: 14.4g

Exciting Peanut Shrimp Curry

Prep Time: 15 minutes.
Cook Time: 10 minutes.
Serves: 4
Ingredients:
- 2 tablespoons Green Curry paste
- 1 cup vegetable stock
- 1 cup coconut milk
- 6 ounces pre-cooked shrimp
- 5 ounces broccoli florets
- 3 tablespoons chopped cilantro
- 2 tablespoons coconut oil
- 1 tablespoon peanut butter
- 1 tablespoon soy sauce
- Juice of ½ lime
- 1 medium-sized spring onion, chopped up
- 1 teaspoon crushed roasted garlic
- 1 teaspoon minced ginger
- 1 teaspoon fish sauce
- ½ teaspoon turmeric
- ¼ teaspoon xanthan gum
- ¼ cup source cream

Preparation:
1. Startup by taking a pan over medium heat and add up 2 tablespoons of coconut oil.
2. Once the oil is melted, toss in the minced ginger and chopped up spring onion. Let them cook for about a minute.
3. Add about 1 tablespoon of soy sauce, peanut butter, and fish sauce and mix them well.
4. Then add in a cup of vegetable stock and just a cup of coconut milk.
5. Stir them well and add the green curry paste and turmeric.
6. Simmer them for a while.
7. Add about ¼ teaspoon of xanthan gum to the curry and mix it properly.
8. After a while, you will notice that the curry will begin to thicken; that will be the moment when you are going to be needing to throw in the florets and stir them finely.
9. Add in the fresh chopped cilantro.
10. Once the consistency is fine, you are going to need to toss the weighed pre-cooked shrimp and add the lime juice.
11. Let the mixture for a few minutes and season it with pepper and salt as required.
12. Finally, serve it hot alongside just ¼ cup of sour cream with each serving.
Serving Suggestion: Serve over a bed of rice; you can go for sticky rice, jasmine rice, or any other rice appropriate for Thai cuisine. You may opt for Thai Fried Rice as well.

Variation Tip: Add banana blossom/basil/chili peppers/cilantro during or after cooking for an additional flavorful punch.
Nutritional Information Per Serving:
Calories 329 | Fat 28g |Sodium 593mg | Carbs 16g | Fiber 2g | Sugar 3g | Protein 8g

Thai Butternut Squash and Chickpea Curry

Preparation Time: 5 minutes
Cooking Time: 16 minutes
Servings: 2
Ingredients:
- 2 tablespoons red curry paste
- 1 tablespoon yellow curry paste
- ½ cup vegetable stock
- ½ cup chopped potatoes
- ¾ cup chickpeas
- 1 tablespoon brown sugar
- ½ tablespoon vegetable oil
- ½ cup coconut milk
- ½ cup cubed butternut squash
- Salt, to taste

Preparation:
1. In a skillet, add oil and heat.
2. Then add red curry paste and yellow curry paste in the skillet and cook for about 1 minute.
3. Add vegetable stock, potatoes, squash, and coconut milk and cook for about 10 minutes, stirring continuously.
4. Add in brown sugar, salt, and chickpeas and cook for about 5 minutes.
5. Remove and serve.
Serving Suggestions: Serve warm with some coriander on the top.
Variation Tip: You can also use olive oil.
Nutritional Information per Serving:
Calories: 601 | Fat: 31.3g|Sat Fat: 15.3g|Carbs: 66.3g|Fiber: 17.4g|Sugar: 15.5g|Protein: 16.8g

Panang Curry

Prep Time: 10 minutes.
Cook Time: 15 minutes.
Serves: 4

Ingredients:
- 2 tablespoons vegetable oil
- 14 ounces boneless chicken thighs (cut into small pieces)
- ½ cup red bell pepper, sliced
- ½ cup yellow bell pepper, sliced
- 1 cup broccoli florets
- 4 tablespoons Panang curry paste
- 1 tablespoon palm sugar
- 5 to 6 Kaffir lime leaves (chopped)
- 2 red bird's eye chilies (chopped)
- 2 cups coconut milk
- 1 cup water, seasoned to taste
- 2 tablespoons fish sauce
- 1 bunch Thai basil

Preparation:
1. Begin by chopping the chicken and vegetables. Wash the chicken breast and cut into 1-inch cubes with a sharp knife. Cut the red bell peppers, and the yellow bell peppers into slices, and a small broccoli head into bite-size florets.
2. In a medium-sized pan, heat 2 tablespoons vegetable oil.
3. Fry the chicken pieces in the pan on high heat for 3-4 minutes or until they are slightly browned.
Note: If making vegan, omit this phase. You may substitute another kind of meat for the chicken.
4. Fry for 2 minutes with 1/2 cup sliced red bell peppers, 1/2 cup sliced yellow bell peppers, and 1 cup tiny broccoli florets.
5. Please keep in mind that you can use any vegetables you want.
6. Place the chicken and vegetables on the pan's side.
7. To the pan, add 4 tablespoons Panang curry paste.
Note: For a vegan version, use vegan Panang curry paste instead of the standard one, which contains shrimp paste. If you prefer a milder curry, reduce the amount of paste used.
8. Fry for 2 minutes before mixing it together.
9. Cook for another minute after adding 1 tbsp palm sugar.
10. Allow the curry to simmer for 10-12 minutes after adding 5-6 sliced Kaffir lime leaves, 2 chopped bird's eye red chilies, and 2 cups coconut milk. Now, add 1 cup of water and thoroughly combine.
11. Mix in 2 tablespoons fish sauce and a bunch of broken Thai basil. To make it vegan, omit the fish sauce and replace it with soy sauce or tamari.
12. Serve immediately.

Serving Suggestion: Serve over a bed of rice; you can go for sticky rice, jasmine rice, or any other rice appropriate for Thai cuisine. You may opt for Thai Fried Rice as well.

Variation Tip: Add banana blossom/basil during or after cooking for an additional flavorful punch.

Nutritional Information Per Serving:
Calories 516 | Fat 31g |Sodium 1405mg | Carbs 15g | Fiber 1g | Sugar 7g | Protein 45g

Thai Red Chicken Curry

Preparation Time: 10 minutes
Cooking Time: 35 minutes
Servings: 8

Ingredients:
- 3 pounds chicken breasts
- 2 red bell peppers, thinly sliced
- 4 garlic cloves, minced
- 4 tablespoons red curry paste
- 6 tablespoons torn cilantro
- 4 tablespoons coconut oil
- 1 tablespoon grated ginger
- 3½ cups coconut milk
- Salt and pepper, to taste

Preparation:
1. Before cooking, heat the oven to 375 degrees F.
2. Add salt and pepper to season and set it aside for later use.
3. In a skillet, add coconut oil and chicken and cook until golden brown.
4. Add pepper, garlic, and ginger and cook for about 2 minutes.
5. Add curry paste and cook for about 5 minute, stirring well.
6. Pour in the coconut milk and mix well.
7. Bake in the preheated oven for about 25 minutes.
8. Take out and add cilantro to garnish.
9. Serve and enjoy!

Serving Suggestions: Top with peanuts and serve.

Variation Tip: You can also use tomatoes to enhance taste.

Nutritional Information per Serving:
Calories: 1503 | Fat: 132.6g|Sat Fat: 108.4g|Carbs: 32g| Fiber: 11.5g|Sugar: 17.8g|Protein: 61.1g

Thai Coconut Garbanzo and Tomato Curry

Cooking Time: 5 minutes
Preparation Time: 11 minutes
Servings: 2
Ingredients:
- 1 tablespoon olive oil
- 1 cup garbanzo, drained
- ½ tablespoon fish sauce
- ½ tablespoon soy sauce
- ½ onion, diced
- 1 tomato, chopped
- ¾ cup coconut milk
- 1 tablespoon brown sugar
- 2 lime leaves

Preparation:
1. In a skillet, add oil and heat. When heated, sauté onion in it.
2. Then add garbanzo and tomato and cook for about 1 minute, stirring well.
3. Then add fish sauce, soy sauce, coconut milk, and brown sugar and cook for about 10 minutes, mixing well to combine.
4. Remove and top with lime leaves.
5. Serve and enjoy!

Serving Suggestions: Garnish with cilantro before serving.
Variation Tip: Olive oil can be replaced with almond oil.

Nutritional Information per Serving:
Calories: 467 | Fat: 30.1g|Sat Fat: 20.2g|Carbs: 47.8g|Fiber: 10.1g|Sugar: 10.7g|Protein: 9.5g

Easy Thai Pumpkin Curry

Preparation Time: 10 minutes
Cooking Time: 17 minutes
Servings: 2
Ingredients:
- ½ tablespoon olive oil
- 1 teaspoon curry powder
- ¾ cup coconut milk
- 3 tablespoons chopped spinach
- ½ onion, chopped
- 2 cups cubed pumpkin
- ½ cup vegetable broth
- ¼ cup cilantro, chopped

Preparation:
1. In a pot, heat oil.
2. Add onion and curry powder and fry for about 2 minutes.
3. Add pumpkin, coconut milk, and broth and cook for about 10 minutes.
4. Then add in spinach and cook for about 5 minutes, stirring well.
5. Remove and add the chopped cilantro on top.
6. Serve and enjoy!

Serving Suggestions: Top with cashews before serving.
Variation Tip: Almond milk can be used instead of coconut milk.

Nutritional Information per Serving:
Calories: 311 | Fat: 25.7g|Sat Fat: 19.7g|Carbs: 20.6g|Fiber: 5.7g|Sugar: 6.9g|Protein: 5.6g

Thai Green Chicken Curry

Preparation Time: 15 minutes
Cooking Time: 17 minutes
Servings: 8
Ingredients:
- 4 tablespoons vegetable oil
- 3½ cups coconut milk
- 2 teaspoons white sugar
- 12 lime leaves
- 4 eggplants, sliced
- 2 cups vegetable broth
- 2 teaspoons fish sauce
- 3 cups sliced chicken thighs
- 3 cups snow peas, trimmed
- 4 tablespoons green curry paste
- 4 cups chopped basil
- 2 tablespoons lime juice
- Salt, to taste

Preparation:
1. In a skillet, heat the vegetable oil.
2. Add the green curry paste and cook for about 3 minutes.
3. Pour in the vegetable broth and coconut milk and stir well.
4. Add fish sauce, sugar, lime leaves, salt, and chicken and cook for about 7 minutes.
5. Then add lime juice, snow peas, and basil leaves and cook for about 2 minutes.
6. Remove and serve! Enjoy!

Serving Suggestions: Squeeze lemon on the top.
Variation Tip: You can also use chicken broth.
Nutritional Information per Serving:
Calories: 1395 | Fat: 124.3g|Sat Fat: 100.9g|Carbs: 61.5g| Fiber: 24.6g|Sugar: 29.3g|Protein: 32.9g

Thai Red Curry Rice Noodles

Preparation Time: 10 minutes
Cooking Time: 10 minutes
Servings: 4
Ingredients:
- 2 cups rice noodles, soaked
- 4 garlic cloves, finely chopped
- 1 cup vegetable broth
- 2 tablespoons maple syrup
- 4 tablespoons red curry paste
- 2 cups coconut milk
- 4 tablespoons soy sauce
- 2 tablespoons lime juice
- Salt, to taste

Preparation:
1. In a skillet, add red curry paste and cook for about 5 minutes.
2. Add garlic and sauté for about 1 minute.
3. Mix together coconut milk, noodles, lime juice, maple syrup, vegetable broth, and soy sauce in the pan and cook for about 4 minutes.
4. Take out and serve. Enjoy!

Serving Suggestions: Top with sesame seeds before serving.
Variation Tip: You can also add green onions to enhance taste.
Nutritional Information per Serving:
Calories: 486 | Fat: 33.7g|Sat Fat: 27g|Carbs: 42.6g|Fiber: 3.8g|Sugar: 10.8g|Protein: 6g

Thai Red Beef Curry

Preparation Time: 15 minutes
Cooking Time: 90 minutes
Servings: 3
Ingredients:
- 1 pound stewing beef, cut into bite-sized pieces
- 1 tablespoon vegetable oil
- ½ tablespoon minced ginger
- 2 cups beef stock
- ½ onion, minced
- 2 garlic cloves, minced
- 2 tablespoons red curry paste
- ½ butternut squash, chopped
- 1 tablespoon lime juice
- ¾ cup coconut milk
- Handful of baby spinach leaves
- Salt and pepper, to taste

Preparation:
1. Toss the beef with salt and pepper to season.
2. In a pan, heat oil. Add the seasoned beef and cook for about 5 minutes.
3. Add curry paste, beef, and beef stock and simmer for about 1 hour.
4. Add in the spinach and cook for about 20 minutes.
5. Pour lime juice and coconut milk and stir well to combine.
6. Take out and serve.

Serving Suggestions: Serve with chopped basil leaves on the top.
Variation Tip: You can also add fish sauce to enhance taste.
Nutritional Information per Serving:
Calories: 538 | Fat: 31.7g|Sat Fat: 18.3g|Carbs: 12.4g|Fiber: 2.4g|Sugar: 3.6g|Protein: 49.8g

Thai Mushroom Tomato Curry

Preparation Time: 10 minutes
Cooking Time: 14 minutes
Servings: 4
Ingredients:
- 2 cups mushrooms
- 1 onion, chopped
- 1 tablespoon tomato puree
- 1 tablespoon vegetable oil
- 1 cup coconut milk
- 1 garlic clove, minced
- 1½ lemongrass stalk, chopped
- Salt, to taste

Preparation:
1. In a blender, blend together onion, tomato puree, garlic lemongrass, and salt to form a smooth puree. Set aside for later use.
2. In a pan, heat oil. Then add puree and cook for about 9 minutes.
3. Add mushrooms and coconut milk and cook for about 5 minutes.
4. Take out and serve.

Serving Suggestions: Serve with chopped coriander on the top.
Variation Tip: Add lime juice for even better taste.
Nutritional Information per Serving:
Calories: 196 | Fat: 17.9g|Sat Fat: 13.4g|Carbs: 9.3g|Fiber: 2.4g|Sugar: 4g|Protein: 3g

Crunchy Thai Salad with Peanut Dressing

Prep Time: 30 minutes.
Serves: 4

Ingredients:

To Go with the Thai Peanut Dressing
• 1 tablespoon smooth peanut butter
• 2 tablespoons rice vinegar, unseasoned
• 2 tablespoons fresh lime juice (from one lime)
• 3 tablespoons vegetable oil
• 1 teaspoon soy sauce (use gluten-free if needed)
• 2 teaspoons honey
• 2 ½ teaspoons sugar
• 2 cloves garlic, finely chopped
• 1-inch square fresh ginger slice, peeled and roughly chopped
• 1 teaspoon sea salt
• a quarter teaspoon crushed red pepper flakes
• 2 tablespoons cilantro leaves, new

To Make the Salad
• 4 cups Napa cabbage chopped or shredded coleslaw mix (I like to toss in a little shredded red cabbage for color)
• 1 cup shredded carrots, prepared
• 1 red bell pepper, thinly sliced and diced into bite-sized pieces
• 1 small English cucumber, halved, seeded, and thinly sliced
• 1 cup edamame, cooked and shelled
• 2 thinly sliced medium scallions
• ½ cup chopped fresh cilantro, loosely packed

Preparation:
1. In a blender, combine all of the dressing ingredients except the cilantro and process until fully smooth. Add the cilantro and pulse for a few seconds or until it is finely chopped. Place in the refrigerator until ready to eat.
2. To make the salad, toss together all of the ingredients in a big mixing bowl. If serving immediately, drizzle the peanut dressing over the top and toss; otherwise, serve the dressing on the side to prevent the salad from being soggy

Serving Suggestion: Serve over a bed of rice; you can go for sticky rice, jasmine rice, or any other rice appropriate for Thai cuisine.

Variation Tip: Add cilantro/coriander/oyster sauce during or after cooking for an additional flavorful punch.

Nutritional Information Per Serving:
Calories 782 | Fat 36g |Sodium 2095mg | Carbs 67g | Fiber 10g | Sugar 6g | Protein 56g

Stir-Fried Baby Mushrooms

Prep Time: 10 minutes.
Cook Time: 15 minutes.
Serves: 4

Ingredients:
• 2 tablespoons olive oil
• 3 garlic cloves, minced
• 1 onion, diced
• 8 ears baby corn, sliced
• ⅔ pound fresh mushrooms, sliced
• 1 tablespoon fish sauce
• 1 tablespoon mild soy sauce
• 1 teaspoon oyster sauce
• 2 tablespoons cornstarch
• 3 tablespoons water
• ¼ cup chopped fresh cilantro
• 1 red chili pepper, sliced

Preparation:
1. In a large skillet or wok, heat the oil over medium heat; cook the garlic in the hot oil until browned, 5 to 7 minutes.
2. Cook until the onion and baby corn are translucent, around 5 to 7 minutes. Cook the mushrooms in the mixture for around 2 minutes or until they are slightly softened.
3. Stir in the fish sauce, soy sauce, and oyster sauce until thoroughly combined.
4. In a small cup, whisk together the cornstarch and water until the cornstarch is dissolved; pour into the mushroom mixture.
5. Cook, constantly stirring until the sauce is thickened and glistening.
6. To eat, move to a serving dish and garnish with chili pepper and cilantro.

Serving Suggestion: Serve with some Sweet Thai Chili Sauce or your desired dipping sauce.

Variation Tip: Add banana blossom/basil/chili peppers/ coriander/oyster sauce during or after cooking for an additional flavorful punch.

Nutritional Information Per Serving:
Calories 223 | Fat 8g |Sodium 286mg | Carbs 34g | Fiber 3g | Sugar 5g | Protein 6g

Lovely Morning Glory Stir Fry (Pad Pak Boong)

Prep Time: 10 minutes.
Cook Time: 2-3 minutes.
Serves: 4

Ingredients:
- 1 pound Morning Glory
- 2-3 Thai chili peppers, new (Or 2 small dried chili peppers)
- 6 garlic cloves

Stir-Fry Sauce
- 1 tablespoon Korean soybean paste (Doenjang) (Miso Paste is also acceptable!)
- 1 teaspoon Mirim (Rice Wine)
- 1 tablespoon oyster sauce
- ½ tablespoon soy sauce
- ½ tablespoon sugar

Additional Ingredient for Stir-Frying
- ½ tablespoon soy sauce
- 3-4 tablespoons cooking oil
- a pinch of water

Preparation:
Preparation Ingredients
1. Clean Morning Glory thoroughly. Set it in a strainer and let the excess water drain. The stems should then be cut into pinky-finger lengths. Then, cut the leafy part into pointer-finger lengths.
2. Remove the garlic cloves' ends. Then get out your mortar and pestle. Pound the garlic cloves (6) and chili peppers (2-3) together gently. After that, set aside.
3. Stir together the following ingredients to make the Stir-fry Sauce: soybean paste (1 tablespoon), Mirim (1 tablespoon), oyster sauce (1 tablespoon), soy sauce (½ tablespoon), and sugar (½ tablespoon). Thoroughly combine all of the ingredients.

Preparing the Meal
1. In a wok or frying pan, heat 3-4 tablespoons cooking oil. Plan on cooking on medium-high heat. When the oil is hot, add the garlic and chili peppers first.
2. Stir-fry until the mixture becomes aromatic. Then add the stems of morning glory. ½ tablespoon soy sauce comes next. For 30 seconds, stir-fry the stems in the soy sauce.
3. Add the leaves after 30 seconds. Then whisk in the rest of the stir-fry sauce.
4. Stir-fry for another 15-20 seconds. Remove from heat and place on a tray.
5. Serve right away with a bowl of hot rice!

Serving Suggestion: Serve over a bed of rice; you can go for sticky rice, jasmine rice, or any other rice appropriate for Thai cuisine. You may opt for Thai Fried Rice as well.

Variation Tip: Add banana blossom/basil/chili peppers/cilantro during or after cooking for an additional flavorful punch.

Nutritional Information Per Serving:
Calories 301 | Fat 22g |Sodium 661mg | Carbs 14g | Fiber 5g | Sugar 7g | Protein 19g

Cool Stir-Fried Vegetable (Pad Pak Ruammit)

Prep Time: 15 minutes.
Cook Time: 10-15 minutes.
Serves: 4

Ingredients:
- ½ cup broccoli
- ½ cup mange tout
- 1 cup baby corn
- ½ cup carrots, sliced
- ½ cup red pepper, sliced
- ½ cup white mushrooms, sliced
- 1 garlic clove, finely chopped
- ½ tablespoon sugar
- 1 tablespoon soy sauce
- 2 tablespoons oyster sauce
- 2 tablespoons water
- 2 tablespoons sesame oil

Preparation:
1. To make the stir fry sauce: In a mixing bowl, combine 2 tablespoons oyster sauce, ½ tablespoon sugar, 1 tablespoon soy sauce, and 2 tablespoons water.
2. Heat 2 tablespoons of sesame oil in a wok over high heat, then add 1 clove finely chopped garlic and ½ cup sliced carrots and stir fry for 1 minute.
3. To the wok, add ½ cup broccoli, ½ cup baby corn, and ½ cup mange tout and stir fry for another minute or so.
4. Add ½ cup sliced red peppers and ½ cup sliced white mushrooms, followed by the sauce we made earlier. Stir all together for a few minutes more, until the vegetables are cooked to your taste, then serve with steamed jasmine rice!

Serving Suggestion: Serve over a bed of rice; you can go for sticky rice, jasmine rice, or any other rice appropriate for Thai cuisine. You may opt for Thai Fried Rice as well.

Variation Tip: Add banana blossom/basil/chili peppers/cilantro/coriander/oyster sauce during or after cooking for an additional flavorful punch.

Nutritional Information Per Serving:
Calories 170 | Fat 15g |Sodium 133mg | Carbs 7g | Fiber 1g | Sugar 3g | Protein 4g

Stir-Fried Bok Choy and Sesame

Prep Time: 10 minutes.
Cook Time: 15 minutes.
Serves: 4
Ingredients:
• 2 large bunch Bok choy, cut off, leaves rinsed
• 1 tablespoon sesame oil
• 1 tablespoon olive oil
• 2 whole eggs
• 2 tablespoons low-carb soy sauce
• 1 tablespoon sesame seeds
Preparation:
1. Take a frying pan and place it over medium heat.
2. When the pan is hot, add the sesame seeds and toast till it turns golden.
3. Add olive oil, sesame oil, and soy sauce, then bring to a simmer.
4. Add the Bok choy and stir to coat in oil and soy sauce.
5. Stir the Bok choy continuously as it cooks and wilts.
6. Once done, remove it from the pan and set it aside.
7. whisk eggs to the pan.
8. Scramble them in the remaining soy sauce and oil till just set.
9. Spoon the scrambled eggs over the Bok choy.
10. Serve and enjoy.
Serving Suggestion: Serve over a bed of rice; you can go for sticky rice, jasmine rice, or any other rice appropriate for Thai cuisine. You may opt for Thai Fried Rice as well.
Variation Tip: Add banana blossom/ oyster sauce during or after cooking for an additional flavorful punch.
Nutritional Information Per Serving:
Calories 114 | Fat 9g |Sodium 558mg | Carbs 10g | Fiber 3g | Sugar 4g | Protein 3g

Thai Stir-Fried Pumpkin Meal (Pad Fuk Thong)

Prep Time: 10 minutes.
Cook Time: 5-10 minutes.
Serves: 4
Ingredients:
• 2 tablespoons olive oil
• 1 teaspoon finely chopped garlic
• 1 cup pork, finely chopped (or other meat or tofu)
• 1 ½ cups (bite-size) peeled pumpkin cubes
• 2 beaten eggs
• 1 tablespoon oyster sauce
• 1 tbsp. light soy sauce (vegetarian if desired)
• 1 tsp Golden Mountain Seasoning Sauce
• 1 tablespoon sugar
• ¼ cup stock (chicken or vegetable)
• ½ cup green onion, 2 inches long
Preparation:
1. In a wok, heat the oil until it is very hot. Stir in the garlic and cook until golden brown. Cook until the meat or tofu is finished.
2. Combine the pumpkin, stock, oyster sauce, soy sauce, seasoning sauce, and sugar in a mixing bowl.
3. Stir all together and cook for 3 minutes, or until the pumpkin is almost cooked.
4. Break the eggs into the wok and stir to combine; add the green onion and remove from the heat.
5. Serve with freshly steamed jasmine rice.
Serving Suggestion: Serve over a bed of rice; you can go for sticky rice, jasmine rice, or any other rice appropriate for Thai cuisine. You may opt for Thai Fried Rice as well.
Variation Tip: Add banana blossom/basil/chili peppers/cilantro/coriander during or after cooking for an additional flavorful punch.
Nutritional Information Per Serving:
Calories 365 | Fat 26g |Sodium 490mg | Carbs 23g | Fiber 4g | Sugar 5g | Protein 11g

Green Papaya Mix (Som Tum)

Prep Time: 15 minutes.
Serves: 4
Ingredients:
• 10 small-sized dried shrimp
• 2 small-sized red Thai chiles
• 1 peeled garlic clove
• ¼ cup tamarind juice
• 1 tablespoon grated palm sugar
• 1 tablespoon Thai fish sauce
• 1 lime cut up into 1-inch pieces
• 4 cherry tomatoes, halved
• 3 long beans, trimmed up into 1-inch pieces
• 1 carrot, shredded
• ½ English cucumber coarsely and seeded
• ⅙ small green cabbage, cored and thinly sliced
• 1 pound unripe green papaya, quartered seeded, and finely shredded using a mandolin
• 3 tablespoons of unsalted roasted peanuts
Preparation:
1. Take a mortar and pestle and crush your shrimp alongside garlic, chiles.

2. Add tamarind juice, fish sauce, and palm sugar.
3. Squeeze 3 quarts of lime pieces over the mortar.
4. Grind to make a dressing.
5. Add the remaining ingredients (excluding the peanut), making sure to add the papaya last.
6. Use the pestle and spoon to grind well.
7. Mix the vegetable and fruit and coat them well.
8. Transfer to your serving dish.
9. Garnish with some peanuts and lime pieces.
10. Enjoy!

Serving Suggestion: Serve over a bed of rice; you can go for sticky rice, jasmine rice, or any other rice appropriate for Thai cuisine. You may opt for Thai Fried Rice as well.

Variation Tip: Add banana blossom/basil /oyster sauce during or after cooking for an additional flavorful punch.

Nutritional Information Per Serving:
Calories 132 | Fat 3g |Sodium 1445mg | Carbs 27g | Fiber 6g | Sugar 16g | Protein 4g

Thai Coconut Corn Fritters

Preparation Time: 10 minutes
Cooking Time: 4 minutes
Servings: 8
Ingredients:
• 4 cups fresh corn kernels
• 6 green onions, thinly sliced
• 6 tablespoons coconut milk
• 2 teaspoons chili garlic sauce
• ½ cup all-purpose flour
• 2 teaspoons baking powder
• ½ cup cilantro, chopped
• 2 eggs
• 4 teaspoons ginger, finely minced
• 4 tablespoons coconut oil
• Salt and pepper, to taste

Preparation:
1. In a bowl, mix together the corn, green onions, coconut milk, chili garlic, eggs, and cilantro.
2. Then add all-purpose flour, baking powder, salt, and pepper and sift properly.
3. In a skillet, add coconut oil. Add the corn mixture and cook for about 2 minutes on each side, flattening the top.
4. Remove the mixture and transfer to a serving plate.
5. Serve and enjoy!

Serving Suggestions: Serve with a dipping sauce.

Variation Tip: You can add red curry paste to enhance taste.
Nutritional Information per Serving:
Calories: 215 | Fat: 11.9g|Sat Fat: 8.8g|Carbs: 25.8g|Fiber: 3.3g|Sugar: 4.8g|Protein: 5.8g

Sesame Garlic Dressing Thai Salad

Prep Time: 15 minutes.
Cook Time: 20 minutes.
Serves: 4
Ingredients:
To make the dressing:
• ⅓ cup canola oil
• 3 garlic cloves, peeled
• 3 tablespoons low-sodium soy sauce
• 2 teaspoons water
• 2 tablespoons distilled white vinegar
• 2 teaspoons honey
• 1 tablespoon sesame seed oil
• 1 tablespoon lemon grass paste (ginger would also work)
• a dash of lime juice
To make the salad:
• 16 ounces shelled frozen edamame
• 5–6 cups kale (baby)
• 3 medium carrots
• 2 red bell peppers (1 red, 1 yellow)
• 1 cup cilantro stems
• 3 green onions
• ¾ cup cashews (Trader Joe's Thai Lime and Chili Cashews are fantastic if you can find them)

Preparation:
1. In a food processor, combine all of the dressing ingredients and puree until smooth. Taste and customize to suit your tastes. Transfer to a dressing jar and rinse the food processor for later use.
2. Boil the edamame for 3-5 minutes in a pot of boiling water. Enable to cool after draining. Meanwhile, thinly slice or shred the kale, carrots, peppers, cilantro leaves, and green onions.
3. In a food processor, pulse the cooked edamame 5 times to get a minced texture. Transfer to a bowl and do the same with the cashews. Toss together the kale, carrots, peppers, cilantro, green onions, edamame, and cashews. Drizzle with the dressing, throw a few times and serve right away.

Serving Suggestion: Serve over a bed of rice; you can go for sticky rice, jasmine rice, or any other rice appropriate for Thai cuisine.

Variation Tip: Add banana blossom during or after cooking for an additional flavorful punch.

Nutritional Information Per Serving:
Calories 86 | Fat 6g |Sodium 443mg | Carbs 6g | Fiber 1g | Sugar 2g | Protein 4g

Maple Baked Sweet Potatoes and Purple Yams

Preparation Time: 5 minutes
Cooking Time: 45 minutes
Servings: 2
Ingredients:
- 1 sweet potato, peeled and cubed
- ½ carrot, chopped
- ¼ teaspoon cayenne pepper
- ½ teaspoon cumin seeds
- 2 purple yams, peeled and cubed
- 1½ tablespoons coconut oil
- ⅛ teaspoon ground cumin
- 1 tablespoon maple syrup

Preparation:
1. Before cooking, heat the oven to 350 degrees F.
2. In a baking dish, add yams, carrots, and sweet potatoes and sprinkle with cumin seeds, ground cumin, coconut oil, and cayenne pepper.
3. Toss well and bake in the preheated baking oven for about 45 minutes.
4. Remove and drizzle maple syrup on top.
5. Serve and enjoy!

Serving Suggestions: Garnish with coriander before serving.
Variation Tip: Salt and black pepper can be added for better taste.
Nutritional Information per Serving:
Calories: 567 | Fat: 37.7g|Sat Fat: 32.4g|Carbs: 57.4g|Fiber: 7.4g|Sugar: 11.4g|Protein: 3.4g

Stir-Fried Spinach with Peanuts and Garlic

Preparation Time: 5 minutes
Cooking Time: 6 minutes
Servings: 1
Ingredients:
- ½ bunch fresh spinach
- 1 tablespoon oyster sauce
- ½ tablespoon sherry
- ½ teaspoon sesame oil
- ¼ cup peanuts, chopped
- 2 garlic cloves, finely chopped
- 2 tablespoons chicken stock
- ½ tablespoon fish sauce
- ½ teaspoon brown sugar
- 1 tablespoon vegetable oil

Preparation:
1. In a bowl, mix together sesame oil, chicken stock, fish sauce, oyster sauce, brown sugar, and sherry.
2. In a pan, add vegetable oil and heat. Then add garlic and fry for about 1 minute.
3. Add spinach and cook for 1 minute, stirring well.
4. Add the sherry mixture and cook for 4 minutes.
5. Remove and add the chopped peanuts on top.
6. Serve and enjoy!

Serving Suggestions: Serve with red chili flakes on the top.
Variation Tip: You can also use stevia instead of sugar.
Nutritional Information per Serving:
Calories: 436 | Fat: 34.6g|Sat Fat: 5.6g|Carbs: 16.6g|Fiber: 7g|Sugar: 4.1g|Protein: 15.3g

Thai Stir-Fried Mixed Vegetables with Garlic

Preparation Time: 5 minutes
Cooking Time: 10 minutes
Servings: 2
Ingredients:
- 2 garlic cloves, minced
- 1 tablespoon chopped carrots
- 1 tablespoon light soy sauce
- ¼ teaspoon vegan Worcestershire sauce
- 2 tablespoons water
- ½ teaspoon vegetable oil
- ½ cup mushroom, chopped
- 6 tablespoons broccoli
- 1 tablespoon dark soy sauce
- ½ teaspoon sugar
- 1 cup white cabbage, shredded

Preparation:

1. In a frying pan, add garlic and fry for 1 minute.
2. Add mushrooms, broccoli, vegetable oil, Worcestershire sauce, water, soy sauce, sugar, and carrots in the pan and cook for about 8 minutes.
3. Then add the shredded cabbage and cook for about 1 minute.
4. Remove from heat and transfer to serving bowls.
5. Serve and enjoy!

Serving Suggestions: Serve with cashews or sesame seeds on the top.

Variation Tip: You can also use almond oil instead of vegetable oil.

Nutritional Information per Serving:
Calories: 95 | Fat: 1.3g|Sat Fat: 0.2g|Carbs: 26.5g|Fiber: 1.6g|Sugar: 19.7g|Protein: 3.8g

Thai Rice Salad with Cashews

Preparation Time: 15 minutes
Servings: 2
Ingredients:
- ½ cup wild and brown rice mix, cooked
- ½ yellow bell pepper, chopped
- 1½ cups kale, roughly chopped
- 2 green onions, thinly sliced
- ½ red bell pepper, chopped
- 1 cup shredded purple cabbage
- ¼ cucumber, chopped
- ¼ cup cashews, roughly chopped
- 2 tablespoons low-sodium soy sauce
- 1 tablespoon sesame oil
- ½ garlic clove, minced
- ½ teaspoon chili flakes
- 1 tablespoon hoisin sauce
- 1 tablespoon rice vinegar
- ½ tablespoon freshly grated ginger

Preparation:
1. In a large bowl, mix together yellow bell pepper, red bell pepper, purple cabbage, cucumber, kale, rice, and green onions.
2. In another bowl, combine sesame oil, minced garlic clove, chili flakes, rice vinegar, hoisin sauce, soy sauce, and ginger until a smooth mixture is formed.
3. Add the dressing over the rice mixture. Then add cashews on top.
4. Serve and enjoy!

Serving Suggestions: Top with lime wedges before serving.

Variation Tip: Hoisin sauce can be omitted.

Nutritional Information per Serving:
Calories: 373 | Fat: 15.7g|Sat Fat: 2.7g|Carbs: 50.8g|Fiber: 6.9g|Sugar: 9.1g|Protein: 12.3g

Thai Bok Choy Stir-fry

Preparation Time: 7 minutes
Cooking Time: 5 minutes
Servings: 2
Ingredients:
- 1 large Bok choy head, chopped
- 2 garlic cloves, minced
- 1 tablespoon soy sauce
- 1 tablespoon sweet chili sauce
- 1 tablespoon lime juice
- ½ tablespoon coconut oil
- 1 tablespoon oyster-flavored sauce
- 1 tablespoon fish sauce
- 1 tablespoon brown sugar

Preparation:
1. In a bowl, mix together soy sauce, garlic cloves, sweet chili sauce, oyster-flavored sauce, brown sugar, and lime juice.
2. In a frying pan, add coconut oil and heat. Then add Bok choy and the soy sauce mixture and cook for about 5 minutes, stirring continuously.
3. Remove and serve.

Serving Suggestions: Squeeze lemon before serving.

Variation Tip: Fish sauce can be omitted.

Nutritional Information per Serving:
Calories: 116 | Fat: 3.9g|Sat Fat: 2.9g|Carbs: 18.2g|Fiber: 2.2g|Sugar: 11.8g|Protein: 4.8g

Thai Rice Salad with Cucumber and Carrot

Preparation Time: 10 minutes
Servings: 8
Ingredients:
- 3 cups long-grain rice, boiled
- 6 tablespoons fish sauce
- ½ cup sugar
- 2 cucumbers, peeled and diced
- 8 scallions, chopped
- 6 tablespoons lime juice
- 4 tablespoons cooking oil
- ¼ teaspoon cayenne
- 6 carrots, grated
- ¾ cup chopped cilantro
- Salt and black pepper, to taste

Preparation:
1. In a large bowl, add fish sauce, sugar, cucumbers, scallions, and rice and combine well.
2. Then mix in oil, lime juice, cayenne, carrots, salt, and pepper.
3. Add the chopped cilantro on top to garnish and let it sit for about 5 minutes.
4. Serve and enjoy!

Serving Suggestions: You can serve with red chili flakes on the top.
Variation Tip: You can omit black pepper.
Nutritional Information per Serving:
Calories: 409 | Fat: 7.4g|Sat Fat: 1.2g|Carbs: 79.7g|Fiber: 3g|Sugar: 17.5g|Protein: 6.9g

Thai-style Mango Salad

Preparation Time: 12 minutes
Servings: 2
Ingredients:
- ½ Thai green mango, thinly sliced
- ½ zucchini, thinly sliced
- ½ red pepper, chopped
- 1 spring onion, finely chopped
- ½ red chili, diced finely
- 1 cup roasted peanuts, roughly chopped
- 1 tablespoon lime juice
- ½ garlic clove, pressed
- ½ teaspoon maple syrup
- ½ tablespoon sesame oil
- 1 tablespoon tamari
- Black pepper, to taste

Preparation:
1. In a bowl, add zucchini, red pepper, onion, red chili, and mango and mix well.
2. In another bowl, stir together the garlic clove, maple syrup, sesame oil, tamari, black pepper, and lime juice.
3. Add the dressing over the mango mixture. Add the roasted peanuts on the top.
4. Serve and enjoy!

Serving Suggestions: Serve with chopped mint leaves on the top.
Variation Tip: You can also use soy sauce to enhance taste.
Nutritional Information per Serving:
Calories: 507 | Fat: 39.6g|Sat Fat: 5.5g|Carbs: 27.1g|Fiber: 8.3g|Sugar: 7.7g|Protein: 21.2g

Savory Green Papaya Salad

Preparation Time: 15 minutes
Servings: 3
Ingredients:
- 2½ tablespoons fresh lime juice
- 1½ tablespoons fish sauce
- 2 garlic cloves, minced
- ½ green papaya, peeled, halved and seeded
- ½ cup chopped fresh cilantro
- ½ Thai red chili, thinly sliced
- 1½ tablespoons palm sugar
- 1 tablespoon dried shrimp, chopped
- 5 cherry tomatoes, halved
- 1 green onion, thinly sliced
- 1 tablespoon salted peanuts, chopped

Preparation:
1. In a bowl, add sugar, lime juice, fish sauce, garlic cloves, and shrimp and whisk well to coat.
2. In a bowl, mix together papaya, cilantro, red chili, green onion, and tomatoes.
3. Whisk together the papaya mixture and the lime juice mixture to combine until well coated.
4. Add the salted peanuts on top.
5. Serve and enjoy!

Serving Suggestions: Garnish with red chili flakes before serving.
Variation Tip: Use oregano to enhance taste.
Nutritional Information per Serving:
Calories: 161 | Fat: 2.6g|Sat Fat: 0.5g|Carbs: 25.4g|Fiber: 3.9g|Sugar: 18.9g|Protein: 11.3g

Coconut Black Beans

Prep Time: 15 minutes.
Cook Time: 30 minutes.
Serves: 4
Ingredients:
• 1 cup coconut milk
• ½ cup palm sugar
• ½ teaspoon salt
• Water as needed
• ½ cup black beans
Preparation:
1. Soak your black beans overnight under 2 cups of water (the key is to ensure that the water level is 2 inches higher than the beans).
2. Take a pot of water and bring it to a boil.
3. Add the beans and boil them for about 25 minutes until they are soft.
4. Remove the heat.
5. Drain them and reserve the bean water.
6. Take another pot and add coconut milk, salt, and palm sugar.
7. Bring the mix to a simmer and keep stirring it constantly to prevent over-boiling.
8. Once the coconut milk starts to look white /yellowish, let it simmer for another 2-4 minutes.
9. Add the beans to the coconut milk and add 1 cup of your bean water.
10. Let it boil again and wait until the milk shows a purple color.
11. Let it boil again and check for sweetness.
12. Serve when done!
Serving Suggestion: Serve with a topping of Ice Cream in addition to the flavor.
Variation Tip: Add some shredded coconut on top for more flavor.

Nutritional Information Per Serving:
Calories 429 | Fat 23g |Sodium 622mg | Carbs 44g | Fiber 17g | Sugar 3g | Protein 15g

Thai Broccoli Stir-fry

Preparation Time: 5 minutes
Cooking Time: 6 minutes
Servings: 1
Ingredients:
• 6 broccoli stalks
• ¼ teaspoon dried crushed chili
• 1½ tablespoons sherry
• ¾ tablespoon oyster sauce
• ¾ tablespoon chopped garlic
• 1½ tablespoons vegetable oil
• 2 tablespoons chicken stock
• 1 teaspoon brown sugar
Preparation:
1. In a cup, mix together oyster sauce, brown sugar, chicken stock, and sherry.
2. In a pan, add vegetable oil and heat. Then add garlic and chili and cook for 1 minute.
3. Add the broccoli and sherry mixture and cook for about 5 minutes, stirring well.
4. Serve and enjoy!
Serving Suggestions: Garnish it with chopped mint leaves before serving.
Variation Tip: You can also add sriracha sauce to enhance taste.
Nutritional Information per Serving:
Calories: 1217 | Fat: 76.7g|Sat Fat: 14.7g|Carbs: 51.4g|Fiber: 14.8g|Sugar: 17.3g|Protein: 16.3g

The Original Noodle Soup (Guawy Teow)

Prep Time: 15 minutes.
Cook Time: 20 minutes.
Serves: 4

Ingredients:
- 500 g (1 pound) fresh big rice noodle
- 2 tablespoons lard (or vegetable oil)
- 2 tablespoons divided vegetable oil
- 10 shelled and deveined tiny prawns/shrimp
- 2 finely chopped garlic cloves
- 1 Chinese sausage / Lup Chong sausage, thinly sliced on the diagonal 5 cm / 2"-piece fried fish cake, thinly sliced
- 20 garlic chives leaves, sliced into 4 sections
- 2 ½ cups bean sprouts
- 2 whisked eggs

The Sauce:
- 5 tablespoons dark soy sauce
- 4 teaspoons mild soy sauce
- 2 tablespoons oyster sauce
- 4 tablespoons kecap Manis (sweet soy sauce)

Preparation:
1. Combine sauce ingredients well.
2. Do not try to pull noodles apart when they are cold and hard; they may split.
3. Place the entire packet in the microwave and heat on high for 1 ½ to 2 minutes, or until warm and pliable but not hot, turning the packet over as required.
4. Handle with care and position 500g/1-pound noodles in a heatproof dish. Noodles that have been trapped together must be separated.
5. If the noodles become cold and brittle before cooking, cover with cling wrap and microwave for 30 seconds (not hot, just warm) to avoid breakage.
6. In a large nonstick skillet, heat 1 tablespoon oil over high heat.
7. When the pan is hot, add the shrimp and cook for 1 ½ minutes, or until just cooked through, before transferring to a bowl.
8. Cook for 1 minute, or until the Chinese sausage and fish cake are caramelized, before adding to the dish.
9. Cook, pressing in the edges to create a dense omelet with 1 tablespoon oil. Once it's set, roughly chop it with a wooden spoon (as seen in the video), then add it to the cup.
10. Cook for about 1 minute, or until the bean sprouts begin to wilt, before adding to the bowl.
11. Pour in the lard. When the lard has melted and begins to smoke, add the garlic and immediately add the noodles. Fold gently four times with a spatula and a wooden spoon (as seen in the video) to distribute the oil in the noodles.
12. Return all of the other ingredients, including the chives and whisked eggs, to the pot. Fold gently twice more, then pour over the whole amount of Sauce.
13. Gently toss 4 to 6 times to distribute the sauce, pausing in between to allow the noodles to caramelize on the edges a little.
14. Remove from the heat and serve right away.
Serving Suggestion: Serve with some sweet chili sauce or soy sauce.
Variation Tip: Add banana blossom/basil/chili peppers/cilantro during or after cooking for an additional flavorful punch.
Nutritional Information Per Serving:
Calories 902 | Fat 56g |Sodium 1455mg | Carbs 29g | Fiber 4g | Sugar 5g | Protein 68g

Coconut Rice (Khao Mun Gati)

Prep Time: 5 minutes.
Cook Time: 15 minutes.
Serves: 4

Ingredients:
- 2 cups jasmine rice, uncooked
- 1 cup coconut milk
- ½ teaspoon salt
- 1 ¾ cups water

Preparation:
1. Rinse the rice well.
2. Take a medium pot and add water, coconut milk, and salt.
3. Place it over medium heat until the salt dissolves.
4. Transfer the rice to the pot.
5. Stir a few times and bring to a boil.
6. Cover the pot and reduce the heat to the lowest setting, and simmer.
7. Keep heating until most of the coconut milk is absorbed for about 15 minutes.
8. Don't open the pot or stir the rice while it's cooking.
9. Remove from the heat, stir a few times with a fork or spatula.
10. Serve and enjoy!
Serving Suggestion: Serve over a bed of rice; you can go for sticky rice, jasmine rice, or any other rice appropriate for Thai cuisine. You may opt for Thai Fried Rice as well.
Variation Tip: Add banana blossom/basil during or after cooking for an additional flavorful punch.
Nutritional Information Per Serving:
Calories 554 | Fat 32g |Sodium 429mg | Carbs 59g | Fiber 3g | Sugar 1g | Protein 8g

Thai Peanut Butter Noodles

Prep Time: 15 minutes.
Cook Time: 10 minutes.
Serves: 4

Ingredients:
- ½ cup chicken broth
- 1 ½ tablespoons minced fresh ginger root
- 3 tablespoons soy sauce
- 1 ½ tablespoons honey
- 3 tablespoons peanut butter
- 2 teaspoons hot chili paste
- 3 garlic cloves, minced
- 8 ounces Udon noodles
- ¼ cup green onions, chopped
- ¼ cup peanut, chopped

Preparation:
1. Take a large-sized pot and add water.
2. Bring it to a boil and add noodles and cook them until they are soft.
3. Drain the noodles.
4. Take a small saucepan and add chicken broth, soy sauce, ginger, peanut butter, chili paste, honey, and garlic.
5. Cook it over medium heat until the peanut butter has fully melted.
6. Add noodles and give it a toss.
7. Garnish it with peanuts and green onions.
8. Serve!

Serving Suggestion: Serve with some sweet chili sauce or soy sauce.

Variation Tip: Add banana blossom/basil/oyster sauce during or after cooking for an additional flavorful punch.

Nutritional Information Per Serving:
Calories 436 | Fat 16g |Sodium 36mg | Carbs 57g | Fiber 7g | Sugar 7g | Protein 20g

Sukothai Pad Thai

Prep Time: 15 minutes.
Cook Time: 20 minutes.
Serves: 4

Ingredients:

- ½ cup white sugar
- ½ cup distilled vinegar
- ¼ cup soy sauce
- 2 tablespoons tamarind sauce
- 1 (12-ounce) pack dried rice noodles
- ½ cup vegetable oil
- 1 ½ teaspoons minced garlic
- 4 pieces eggs
- 1 (12-ounce) pack firm tofu, cut into ½-inch strips
- 1 ½ tablespoons white sugar
- 1 ½ teaspoons salt
- 1 ½ cups ground peanuts
- 1 ½ teaspoons ground dried oriental radish
- ½ cup chopped fresh chives
- 1 tablespoon paprika
- 2 cups fresh bean sprouts
- 1 lime, cut into wedges

Preparation:
1. To make Pad Thai Sauce: take a saucepan and place it over medium heat.
2. Add sugar, vinegar, soy sauce, and tamarind sauce and blend them well.
3. Soak noodles under cold water until they are tender.
4. Take a large-sized skillet and place it over medium heat.
5. Add oil and warm it.
6. Add garlic and eggs, cook and scramble the egg.
7. Add tofu and stir well until mixed.
8. Add noodles and stir cook.
9. Stir in Pad Thai sauce, 1 and a ½ teaspoon of salt, and 1 and a ½ tablespoon of white sugar.
10. Stir in peanuts and ground radish.
11. Remove the heat and add paprika and chives.
12. Stir for a while and serve with bean sprouts and lime.

Serving Suggestion: Serve with some sweet chili sauce or soy sauce.

Variation Tip: Add banana blossom/basil/chili peppers during or after cooking for an additional flavorful punch.

Nutritional Information Per Serving:
Calories 260 | Fat 30g |Sodium 1345mg | Carbs 75g | Fiber 3g | Sugar 15g | Protein 16g

Thai-Style Stir-Fried Macaroni (Pad Macaroni)

Prep Time: 10 minutes.
Cook Time: 15 to 20 minutes.
Serves: 4

Ingredients:
- 9 ounces chicken breast, pork, or shrimp cut into bite-size pieces
- 3 scallions, cut into 2-inch lengths, white parts also halved lengthwise, kept separate
- 9 ounces macaroni

- 3 tablespoons ketchup
- ½ carrot, peeled and cut crosswise into thin slices
- 2 garlic cloves, finely minced
- 1 onion, cut into ¼ -inch slices
- 1 to 2 tablespoons Sriracha sauce
- 1 large egg
- 2 tomatoes, cored and each cut into 8 wedges
- 1 tablespoon soy sauce
- 2 teaspoons fish sauce
- 2 tablespoons vegetable oil
- Ground white pepper for serving

Preparation:
1. Take a large pot of water over high heat to boil for the pasta.
2. When the water reaches a rolling boil, and adds a pinch of salt and the pasta.
3. Cook the pasta until just about 1 minute short of al dente.
4. Drain well, rinse in cold running water, and set aside.
5. Take a small bowl and add ketchup, Sriracha, soy sauce, and fish sauce.
6. Mix them well and set them aside.
7. Take a large skillet over high heat, then heat the oil until shimmering.
8. Add the garlic and stir-fry until lightly golden for 30 seconds to 1 minute.
9. Add the onion and carrot, and continue to stir-fry until the vegetables are softened.
10. Cook for 2 to 3 minutes.
11. Add the chicken and scallion whites and continue stir-frying until the meat is browned.
12. Then the scallion whites are softened for 3 to 4 minutes.
13. Push all the ingredients to the sides of the wok or skillet with a wooden spoon.
14. Break the egg into the middle of the skillet and lightly scramble it for about 30 seconds.
15. Add the cooked pasta and sauce and toss everything well.
16. Add the tomatoes and scallion greens and continue stir-frying for about 1 minute.
17. Add a sprinkle of white pepper on top.
18. Serve and enjoy!

Serving Suggestion: Serve with some sweet chili sauce or soy sauce.

Variation Tip: Add banana blossom/basil/chili peppers/cilantro/coriander/oyster sauce during or after cooking for an additional flavorful punch.

Nutritional Information Per Serving:
Calories 774 | Fat 38g |Sodium 1530mg | Carbs 57g | Fiber 3g | Sugar 10g | Protein 51g

Pad Thai

Prep Time: 10 minutes.
Cook Time: 10 minutes.
Serves: 4

Ingredients:
- 12 medium raw shrimp, peeled and deveined, tails left on
- 4 ounces thin rice noodles, dried
- 2 eggs
- 2 cups bean sprouts, divided
- 3 tablespoons palm sugar, light brown sugar, or granulated sugar
- 3 scallions, green parts only, cut into 1 and ½ -inch lengths
- ¼ cup fish sauce
- 2 tablespoons shallot, minced
- 1 tablespoon garlic, minced
- 1 to 2 tablespoons water or broth, if needed
- ½ cup pressed tofu or bean curd, cut into ¼ -inch by ¼ -inch by 2-inch slices
- ¼ cup roasted peanuts plus more for serving, slightly crushed in a mortar and pestle or roughly chopped
- 2 tablespoons tamarind paste
- 3 tablespoons vegetable oil, divided
- Lime wedges, for serving

Preparation:
1. Take a large pot of water to boil over high heat.
2. When boiling, turn off the heat.
3. Add the noodles, then stir a few times and let sit for 5 minutes.
4. Rinse the noodles well under cold water and drain well.
5. Use your finger to separate them.
6. Take a small bowl and add fish sauce, palm sugar, and tamarind paste.
7. Mix them well and set them aside.
8. Take a large skillet over medium heat.
9. Heat 1 tablespoon of oil.
10. Add the shrimp and stir-fry just until pink and opaque, 2 to 3 minutes.
11. Remove the shrimp from the wok or skillet with a mesh skimmer or slotted spoon and set aside.
12. Heat the remaining 2 tablespoons of oil in the skillet and add the shallot and garlic.
13. Stir-fry until fragrant and slightly golden, 30 seconds to 1 minute.
14. Add the noodles and sauce mixture, and stir-fry until well-combined and the noodles are soft but not mushy about 1 minute.
15. Add 1 to 2 tablespoons water or broth if the noodles are not soft enough.
16. Push the noodles to the sides of the wok or skillet with a wooden spoon or spatula.
17. Crack the eggs into the middle of the wok or skillet, and scramble with a wooden spoon just until nearly set, about 30 seconds.
18. Add the cooked shrimp, 1 cup bean sprouts, and the tofu, scallions, and peanuts, and toss to combine.
19. Add the lime wedges, the remaining 1 cup bean sprouts, and additional peanuts to sprinkle on top.
20. Serve and enjoy!

Serving Suggestion: Serve with some sweet chili sauce or soy sauce.

Variation Tip: Add Banana Blossom/Oyster Sauce during or after cooking for an additional flavorful punch.

Nutritional Information Per Serving:
Calories 748 | Fat 23g |Sodium 689mg | Carbs 95g | Fiber 5g | Sugar 4g | Protein 32g

Pineapple Fried Rice with Curry Powder and Shrimp (Khao Pad Sapparot)

Prep Time: 10 minutes.
Cook Time: 5 minutes.
Serves: 4

Ingredients:
• 10 medium raw shrimp, peeled and deveined, tails left on
• 2 cups cooked rice, at room temperature (preferably day-old)
• 2 teaspoons curry powder
• 1 egg
• 2 teaspoons fish sauce
• 2 tablespoons vegetable oil
• 1 tablespoon garlic, minced
• ½ cup cashew nuts, roasted
• ¼ cup onion, very thinly sliced
• 2 lime wedges
• 1 cup fresh pineapple, 1-inch chunks
• 2 scallions, cut into ¼ -inch slices
• 1 tablespoon soy sauce
• 2 tablespoons fresh cilantro leaves
• Pinch sugar, granulated

Preparation:
1. Take a small bowl and add soy sauce, fish sauce, curry powder, and sugar.
2. Mix them well and keep them aside.
3. Take a large skillet and add oil, then place it over medium heat.
4. Add the garlic and stir-fry until fragrant, 30 seconds to 1 minute.
5. Then add the onion.
6. Cook until fragrant and the onion is softened for about 30 seconds.
7. Crack the egg into the center of the wok or skillet
8. Stir with a wooden spoon or spatula to mix the egg and yolk well, about 30 seconds.
9. Add the rice, and stir-fry until it is evenly mixed with the egg, about 1 minute.
10. Add the sauce mixture, cashews, scallions, and pineapple.
11. Stir-fry for 30 seconds longer.
12. Add sprinkled with cilantro and with lime wedges for squeezing over each portion.
13. Serve and enjoy!

Serving Suggestion: Serve over a bed of rice; you can go for sticky rice, jasmine rice, or any other rice appropriate for Thai cuisine. You may opt for Thai Fried Rice as well.

Variation Tip: Add banana blossom/ oyster sauce during or after cooking for an additional flavorful punch.

Nutritional Information Per Serving:
Calories 207 | Fat 3g |Sodium 406mg | Carbs 46g | Fiber 3g | Sugar 38g | Protein 3g

Tom Yum Fried Rice with Shrimp (Khao Pad Tom Yum)

Prep Time: 10 minutes.
Cook Time: 5 minutes.
Serves: 4

Ingredients:
• 30 wonton wrappers
• 1 pound peeled, deveined, tail-on raw shrimp (about 30)
• Neutral oil, such as peanut or refined coconut oil, for frying
• Sweet Chili Sauce

Preparation:
1. Clean your work surface and place the wrappers.
2. Use your finger to straighten out each shrimp a bit and place it at the edge of one of the wrappers, leaving the tail off the wrapper.
3. Bring the remaining wrapper all the way over to cover the shrimp.
4. Then, use your thumbs to grab the edge on which the shrimp is lying and roll up to form a cylinder.
5. Use water at the tip of your finger to seal the wrapper.
6. Take a deep skillet over medium-high heat, heat 1 inch of oil to 375 degrees F.
7. Fry the rolls in batches.
8. Be careful not to overcrowd them, just until crisp and golden brown, 1 to 2 minutes.
9. Drain well on paper towels and serve with chili sauce for dipping.
10. Serve and enjoy!

Serving Suggestion: Serve over a bed of rice; you can go for sticky rice, jasmine rice, or any other rice appropriate for Thai cuisine. You may opt for Thai Fried Rice as well.

Variation Tip: Add Banana Blossom/Oyster Sauce during or after cooking for an additional flavorful punch.

Nutritional Information Per Serving:
Calories 182 | Fat 6g |Sodium 436mg | Carbs 24g | Fiber 1g | Sugar 0g | Protein 7g

Sweet and Spicy Coconut Mango Rice

Prep Time: 60 minutes.
Cook Time: 10 minutes.
Serves: 4
Ingredients:
• 1 cup sticky rice
• 1 ¾ cups water
• 1 can coconut cream
• 2 cups white sugar
• 1 pinch salt
• 2 teaspoons corn starch dissolved in 2 tablespoons of water
• 2 ripe mangoes cut up into bite-sized portions
Preparation:
1. Soak the sticky rice in 1 cup of water and allow them to soak for about 60 minutes.
2. Add ¾ cup of water to the rice and bring it to a boil over high heat.
3. Lower down the heat to low and cover with a lid.
4. Take a saucepan and add ¾ cup of coconut cream and place it over medium heat.
5. Allow it to simmer while adding sugar, keep stirring it until the sugar dissolves fully.
6. Once the rice is ready, pour the coconut sauce onto the sticky rice.
7. Remove the heat and cover with your lid for about 15 minutes.
8. Pour ¼ cup of coconut cream into the saucepan and allow it to simmer with salt and cornstarch.
9. Assemble on a serving platter by adding the mango pieces, sticky rice and pour over the coconut cream.
10. Enjoy!
Serving Suggestion: Serve with a topping of Ice Cream if desired.
Variation Tip: Add Chili Peppers/Cilantro/ during or after cooking for an additional flavorful punch.
Nutritional Information Per Serving:
Calories 789 | Fat 30g |Sodium 1346mg | Carbs 127g | Fiber 4g | Sugar 4g | Protein 7g

Green Curry Fried Rice (Khao Pad Gaeng Kiew Wan)

Prep Time: 5 minutes.
Cook Time: 5 minutes.
Serves: 4
Ingredients:
• 4 ounces of any boneless meat (such as pork or chicken), cut against the grain into thin, bite-size pieces (about ¼ inch by 2 to 3 inches)
• ½ cup green peas, fresh or frozen
• 2 cups cooked rice, at room temperature (preferably day-old)
• 2 tablespoons Green Curry Paste
• 2 tablespoons vegetable oil
• 1 tablespoon water, if needed
• 2 teaspoons fish sauce
• 1 teaspoon palm sugar or granulated sugar
• 2 fresh kaffir lime leaves, center ribs removed and julienned, optional
• 1 cup fresh Thai sweet or Italian sweet basil leaves, optional
Preparation:
1. Take a large skillet over medium heat.
2. Heat the oil.
3. Add the curry paste and stir-fry until fragrant for about 1 minute.
4. Add the water if needed, fish sauce, and sugar.
5. Stir-fry until the sugar dissolves, about 30 seconds.
6. Add the meat and peas, and stir-fry until the meat is no longer pink for 3 to 4 minutes.
7. Add the rice and kaffir lime leaves and stir-fry for about 1 minute.
8. Turn off the heat and stir in the basil leaves just until wilted.
9. Serve immediately and enjoy!
Serving Suggestion: Serve over a bed of rice; you can go for sticky rice, jasmine rice, or any other rice appropriate for Thai cuisine.
Variation Tip: Add banana blossom/basil/chili peppers during or after cooking for an additional flavorful punch.
Nutritional Information Per Serving:
Calories 495 | Fat 7g |Sodium 1605mg | Carbs 101g | Fiber 10g | Sugar 29g | Protein 13g

Thai Pork Meatball Skewers

Preparation Time: 15 minutes
Cooking Time: 30 minutes
Servings: 2
Ingredients:
- ½ pound minced pork
- ½ cup steamed rice
- ½ tablespoon ground black pepper
- ½ garlic head, minced
- Salt, to taste

Preparation:
1. In a bowl, add garlic, rice, salt, pork, and pepper and mix well.
2. Divide the mixture and form them into balls. Place into a zip-lock bag.
3. Let the meat balls to ferment at room temperature for 72 hours.
4. On skewers, thread the meat balls.
5. Grill the skewers for 30 minutes.
6. Serve and enjoy!

Serving Suggestions: Serve with chilies on the top.
Variation Tip: Cayenne pepper can be used to enhance taste.

Nutritional Information per Serving:
Calories: 336 | Fat: 4.3g|Sat Fat: 1.5g|Carbs: 38.3g|Fiber: 1g|Sugar: 0.1g|Protein: 33.2g

Thai Fried Turmeric Pork Fillet with Garlic

Preparation Time: 15 minutes
Cooking Time: 10 minutes
Servings: 4
Ingredients:
- 1 pound sliced pork fillet
- 10 garlic cloves, minced
- 1 teaspoon black peppercorn
- 2 tablespoons fresh turmeric
- Salt, to taste

Preparation:
1. In a blender, add turmeric root, black peppercorn, salt, and garlic cloves and blend to form a smooth mixture.
2. Add the pork slices in the mixture and combine well to marinade.
3. Allow the pork to sit for 30 minutes.
4. Then fry until golden brown.
5. Transfer to a serving plate. Serve and enjoy!

Serving Suggestions: Top it with red chili sauce before serving.
Variation Tip: Add black cumin to enhance taste.

Nutritional Information per Serving:
Calories: 289 | Fat: 14.8g|Sat Fat: 5.5g|Carbs: 5g|Fiber: 1g|Sugar: 0.2g|Protein: 32.4g

Thai Shrimp and Sweetcorn Cakes

Preparation Time: 15 minutes
Cooking Time: 10 minutes
Servings: 4
Ingredients:
- 2 cups sweetcorn
- 2 eggs
- 4 tablespoons chopped coriander
- 2 tablespoons soy sauce
- 2 cups all-purpose flour
- 1 cup peeled shrimp
- 6 garlic cloves, minced
- 6 tablespoons oyster sauce
- Salt and black pepper, to taste

Preparation:
1. In a bowl, add shrimp, garlic, and coriander and mix well.
2. Beat eggs and add flour, sweetcorn, pepper, oyster sauce, soy sauce, and salt. Whisk well.
3. Fry the mixture until golden brown.
4. Remove to a serving bowl. Serve and enjoy!

Serving Suggestions: Serve with sweet chili sauce.
Variation Tip: Add sesame seeds to enhance the taste.

Nutritional Information per Serving:
Calories: 365 | Fat: 4.1g|Sat Fat: 1g|Carbs: 65.5g|Fiber: 4g|Sugar: 3g|Protein: 17.5g

Thai Pork on Toast

Preparation Time: 20 minutes
Cooking Time: 30 minutes
Servings: 4
Ingredients:
- 14 bread slices
- 2 tablespoons chopped coriander stalks
- 1 tablespoon soy sauce
- ½ teaspoon brown sugar
- ½ pound minced pork
- 4 garlic cloves, minced
- 1 egg
- 1 teaspoon corn flour
- 2 tablespoons coriander leaves
- Salt, to taste

Preparation:
1. Before cooking, heat the baking oven to 150 degrees F.
2. In a blender, process the garlic cloves and coriander stalks until well blended.
3. In a bowl, beat the egg and add pork. Whisk together to coat.
4. Add sugar, coriander paste, corn flour, soy sauce, and salt in the egg mixture and mix well.
5. Spread the mixture on bread slices and add coriander leaves on top.
6. Toast the slices in baking oven for about 30 minutes.
7. Remove and serve. Enjoy!

Serving Suggestions: Serve with a dipping sauce.
Variation Tip: You can also use palm sugar.
Nutritional Information per Serving:
Calories: 191 | Fat: 4.2g|Sat Fat: 1.3g|Carbs: 18.2g|Fiber: 0.9g|Sugar: 1.9g|Protein: 19.1g

Savory Thai Popcorn

Preparation Time: 12 minutes
Cooking Time: 15 minutes
Servings: 12
Ingredients:

- 4 tablespoons olive oil
- 3 cups salted peanuts, roughly chopped
- 1 cup un-popped popcorns
- ½ cup almond oil
- 4 tablespoons soy sauce
- 2 tablespoons lime zest
- ½ teaspoon baking soda
- 1¼ cups brown sugar
- 6 tablespoons sriracha sauce
- 2 tablespoons lime juice

Preparation:
1. In a large pan, add olive oil and the un-popped popcorn kernels and stir well.
2. Cover the lid of the pan and cook for about 10 minutes until all the popcorn kernel are popped.
3. In another pan, mix together almond oil, brown sugar, soy sauce, lime juice, lime zest, and sriracha and simmer for about 5 minutes.
4. Mixed in the baking soda and the salted peanuts.
5. Serve the popcorns with the sauce mixture.
6.

Serving Suggestions: Garnish cilantro on the top before serving.
Variation Tip: You can add some grated ginger for additional flavor.
Nutritional Information per Serving:
Calories: 461 | Fat: 31.8g|Sat Fat: 3.9g|Carbs: 40.2g|Fiber: 3.4g|Sugar: 34g|Protein: 9.9g

Thai-style Sesame-Peanut Brittle

Preparation Time: 19 minutes
Cooking Time: 20 minutes
Servings: 8
Ingredients:
- ½ cup granulated sugar
- ¾ cup toasted peanuts, chopped
- 2 tablespoons water
- ½ tablespoon vinegar
- ¼ cup sesame seeds, toasted
- Salt, to taste

Preparation:
1. In a pan, add water, sugar, and vinegar and cook for about 12 minutes.
2. Prepare a baking sheet and line over with parchment paper.
3. When the syrup gets hard, add peanuts and sesame seeds. Mix well.
4. Place the syrup on the parchment paper and flatten with a rolling pin.
5. Cut into rectangles, as you desired.
6. Serve and enjoy!

Serving Suggestions: Top with maple syrup before serving.
Variation Tip: Vinegar can be replaced with lemon juice.
Nutritional Information per Serving:
Calories: 150 | Fat: 9g|Sat Fat: 1.3g|Carbs: 15.8g|Fiber: 1.7g|Sugar: 13.1g|Protein: 4.3g

Savory Stir-Fried Shrimp and Sprouts

Preparation Time: 10 minutes
Cooking Time: 5 minutes
Servings: 4
Ingredients:
- 2 cups Brussels sprouts, halved
- 4 garlic cloves, finely chopped
- 2 tablespoons fish sauce
- 2 tablespoons soy sauce
- 2 cups peeled shrimp
- 4 tablespoons oyster sauce
- 2 teaspoons sugar

Preparation:
1. In a pan, boil the Brussels sprouts.
2. Take out the Brussels sprouts and heat oil.
3. Add garlic cloves and the Brussels sprouts in the pan and fry for about 2 minutes.
4. Then add the shrimp, soy sauce, fish sauce, and sugar and fry for 2 more minutes.
5. Take out and serve.
Serving Suggestions: Top with chopped coriander before serving.
Variation Tip: You can also use vinegar to enhance taste.
Nutritional Information per Serving:
Calories: 91 | Fat: 0.9g|Sat Fat: 0.3g|Carbs: 9g|Fiber: 1.8g|Sugar: 3.5g|Protein: 12.4g

Tasty Thai Sweet and Sour Tofu

Preparation Time: 5 minutes
Cooking Time: 25 minutes
Servings: 2
Ingredients:
- ¾ cup tofu, drained, pressed and sliced
- 1½ scallions, chopped
- 1 bell pepper, chopped
- 2 tablespoons tapioca flour
- 2½ tablespoons water
- ½ tablespoon tamari
- 1½ tablespoons brown sugar
- 1½ tablespoons rice vinegar
- ½ tablespoon ketchup
- ¼ teaspoon red pepper flakes

Preparation:
1. In a bowl, mix together the rice vinegar, tamari, ketchup, red pepper flakes, water, and sugar.
2. Toss tofu together with the mixture.
3. In a skillet, fry tofu. Then add scallion, flour, and bell pepper and cook for about 25 minutes, stirring well.
4. When cooked, transfer to a serving plate.
5. Serve and enjoy!
Serving Suggestions: Serve with sesame seeds on the top.
Variation Tip: You can also add honey for a better taste.
Nutritional Information per Serving:
Calories: 607 | Fat: 4.2g|Sat Fat: 0.8g|Carbs: 125.7g|Fiber: 3.8g|Sugar: 29.5g|Protein: 9.7g

Thai Fruit Skewers with Coconut

Preparation Time: 15 minutes
Servings: 16
Ingredients:
- 1 cup reduced-fat coconut milk
- ¼ teaspoon cayenne pepper
- 8 pineapple pieces
- 8 mango slices
- 8 papaya slices
- ½ cup shredded coconut, toasted
- 2 tablespoons finely shredded lime peel
- 4 kiwis, peeled and quartered
- ½ cup fresh mint

Preparation:
1. In a bowl, add cayenne pepper, lime peel, and co-conut milk and mix well.

2. Then add kiwi, pineapple pieces, papaya slices, and mango slices in the bowl and toss together to coat. Cover the bowl and let it sit for 4 hours to strain the mixture.

3. On skewers, thread the fruit alternately and then sprinkle with shredded coconut and fresh mint.

4. Serve and enjoy!

Serving Suggestions: Serve with honey on the top.

Variation Tip: You can also add chia seeds in the mixture.

Nutritional Information per Serving:
Calories: 180 | Fat: 5.2g|Sat Fat: 4.1g|Carbs: 36.2g|Fiber: 5.3g|Sugar: 27.6g|Protein: 2.3g

Thai Avocado Pinwheels

Preparation Time: 15 minutes
Servings: 12
Ingredients:
- 2 tortillas
- 4 tablespoons grated carrot
- 1 avocado, sliced
- 6 tablespoons cilantro
- 1 fresh red pepper
- ½ cup peanut butter
- 1 teaspoon sriracha
- 2 teaspoons brown rice vinegar
- ½ cup sweet red chili sauce
- 1 teaspoon tamari
- 2 tablespoons lime juice

Preparation:
1. In a bowl, add sweet red chili sauce, sriracha, tamari, brown rice vinegar, lime juice, and peanut butter and mix well.

2. On each tortilla, spread the sauce mixture, cilantro, avocado, red pepper, and carrot. Roll tightly and use a knife to slice.

3. Serve and enjoy!

Serving Suggestions: Garnish with chopped mint leaves before serving.

Variation Tip: You can omit sriracha.

Nutritional Information per Serving:
Calories: 197 | Fat: 14.2g|Sat Fat: 3g|Carbs: 13.9g|Fiber: 2.9g|Sugar: 6.9g|Protein: 6.1g

Fresh Spring Rolls (Poh Piah Sod)

Prep Time: 15 minutes.
Cook Time: 10 minutes.
Serves: 4

Ingredients:
- 3 ounces rice-vermicelli noodles, thin
- 8 round, dried rice paper spring roll sheets
- 8 shrimp, cooked, peeled, and halved lengthwise
- ½ cup carrot, grated
- ½ cup bean sprouts
- ¼ cup fresh mint leaves
- ¼ cup fresh cilantro leaves
- 2 or 3 scallions, green parts only, cut into 4-inch lengths

Preparation:
1. Take a small pot to add water so that it covers the vermicelli noodles.

2. Cover it and bring it to a boil over high heat.

3. Plunge the noodles into the boiling water to cover.

4. Then take them off the heat and set them for 6 to 8 minutes.

5. Rinse them well in cold running water and set them aside.

6. Arrange all ingredients in small bowls, then fill a shallow pan with very hot water.

7. Dip each rice paper sheet into the hot water and turn it in a circular motion.

8. Shake off any excess water.

9. Take a large plate or tray, then place the softened rice sheet into it.

10. Place 2 shrimp halves, pink-side down in the middle of the lower third of the sheet.

11. Arrange about ¼ cup of the vermicelli noodles in a cylindrical shape on top of the shrimp.

12. Add bean sprouts and carrots on top of the noodles.

13. Then 3 or 4 mint leaves and 3 or 4 cilantro leaves, and then one of the scallion sections.

14. Roll the rice sheets from the bottom up and tucking them tightly around the filling.

15. Halfway rolled, firmly fold in the left and right sides of the sheet to form an envelope shape.

16. Keep rolling, and then place the finished roll on the tray seam-side down.

17. Let it dry for 5 to 10 minutes before you serve.

18. Serve and enjoy!

Serving Suggestion: Serve with your desired dipping sauce. You may go for garlic sauce, soy sauce, Thai sweet Chili Sauce, and so on.

Variation Tip: Add banana blossom/basil /oyster sauce during or after cooking for an additional flavorful punch.

Nutritional Information Per Serving:
Calories 136 | Fat 3g |Sodium 756mg | Carbs 24g | Fiber 3g | Sugar 10g | Protein 3g

Thai Coffee Candied Peanuts with Sesame Seeds

Preparation Time: 10 minutes
Cooking Time: 25 minutes
Servings: 6
Ingredients:
- 2 cups peanuts
- 2 teaspoons cocoa powder
- ½ cup coconut milk
- 1½ cups sugar
- 2 teaspoons coffee
- ½ cup water
- 4 tablespoons sesame seeds, toasted
- Salt, to taste

Preparation:
1. In a large pan, mix together sugar, cocoa powder, coffee, coconut milk, salt, and water and bring to a boil.
2. Then add peanuts and cook for about 25 minutes.
3. Transfer to serving plates. Add sesame seeds on top to garnish.
4. Then place in the refrigerator for 2 hours.
5. Serve and enjoy!

Serving Suggestions: Serve with maple syrup on top.
Variation Tip: Chocolate syrup can be used to enhance taste.
Nutritional Information per Serving:
Calories: 1045 | Fat: 31.8g|Sat Fat: 8g|Carbs: 194g|Fiber: 5.5g|Sugar: 186g|Protein: 14.2g

Hearty Banana Fries

Prep Time: 15 minutes.
Cook Time: 15 minutes.
Serves: 4
Ingredients:
- ¾ cup white rice flour
- ¼ cup tapioca flour
- 2 tablespoons white sugar
- 1 teaspoon salt
- ½ cup shredded coconut
- 1 ¼ cups water
- 10 bananas, sliced
- 3 cups oil for frying

Preparation:
1. Take a medium-sized bowl and add rice flour, salt, coconut, and tapioca flour.
2. Mix well.
3. Stir in water a bit at a time and keep mixing it until a thick batter form.
4. Peel the bananas and cut them into lengthwise 3-4 pieces.
5. Take a deep fryer and add oil, and allow it to heat up.
6. Coat the banana slices in the batter and fry them until golden.
7. Allow them to drain on a kitchen towel, serve and enjoy!

Serving Suggestion: Serve with a topping of Ice Cream for extra flavor; you may drizzle a bit of chocolate syrup as well.
Variation Tip: Add some shredded coconut on top!
Nutritional Information Per Serving:
Calories 200 | Fat 10g |Sodium 119mg | Carbs 28g | Fiber 1g | Sugar 12g | Protein 3g

Authentic Thai Cashews

Preparation Time: 15 minutes
Cooking Time: 20 minutes
Servings: 4
Ingredients:
- 2 tablespoons coconut oil
- 4 teaspoons Thai red curry paste
- 2 teaspoons ground coriander
- ½ teaspoon ground turmeric
- 2 tablespoons coconut palm sugar
- 4 tablespoons raw sesame seeds
- 4 tablespoons honey
- 2 teaspoons lime juice
- 1 teaspoon ground ginger
- ¼ teaspoon ground cayenne
- 4 cups raw cashews
- Salt, to taste

Preparation:
1. Before cooking, heat the baking oven to 350 degrees F.

2. Prepare a baking sheet and line parchment paper over.
3. In a bowl, mix together the honey, coconut oil, red curry paste, lime juice, turmeric, and ginger.
4. Season with cayenne pepper, salt, sugar, salt, and sesame seeds and stir well to combine.
5. Then add cashews in the bowl and toss well.
6. Bake the cashews in the preheated oven for about 20 minutes.
7. When cooked, remove from the oven.
8. Serve and enjoy!
Serving Suggestions: Garnish with chopped mint leaves before serving.
Variation Tip: Turmeric can be omitted.
Nutritional Information per Serving:
Calories: 1011 | Fat: 76.3g|Sat Fat: 19.6g|Carbs: 73.6g|Fiber: 5.4g|Sugar: 29g|Protein: 22.8g

Baked Dried Mushrooms

Preparation Time: 25 minutes
Cooking Time: 40 minutes
Servings: 4
Ingredients:
• 2 cups mushrooms, thinly sliced
• 2 tablespoons water
• 2 tablespoons sesame seeds
• 2 tablespoons palm sugar
• 2 teaspoons soy sauce
• Salt, to taste
Preparation:
1. Before cooking, heat the baking oven to 200 degrees F.
2. Prepare a baking tray and place the mushroom slices evenly. Then bake in the preheated oven for about 30 minutes.
3. While cooking the mushrooms, mix together sesame seeds, soy sauce, salt, and palm sugar in a bowl.
4. Then add the cooked mushrooms in the mixture and stir well.
5. Bake the mushrooms again for about 10 minutes.
6. Serve and enjoy!
Serving Suggestions: Top with maple syrup before serving.

Variation Tip: Soy sauce can be replaced with fish sauce.
Nutritional Information per Serving:
Calories: 43 | Fat: 2.3g|Sat Fat: 0.3g|Carbs: 4.4g|Fiber: 0.9g|Sugar: 2.6g|Protein: 2.1g

Thai Crusted Shrimp Cake

Preparation Time: 10 minutes
Cooking Time: 8 minutes
Servings: 2
Ingredients:
• ½ cup breadcrumbs
• 1 tablespoon minced green onion
• 1 teaspoon fish sauce
• ¾ teaspoon minced ginger
• 1 egg
• ¼ pound shrimp, peeled, deveined and chopped
• 2 tablespoons dried coconut
• 1 tablespoon fresh cilantro, chopped
• 1 tablespoon sriracha sauce
• ½ teaspoon lime juice
• ½ garlic clove, minced
• ½ tablespoon olive oil
Preparation:
1. In a bowl, add coconut, breadcrumbs, green onions, cilantro, fish sauce, ginger, sriracha sauce, lime juice, beaten egg, and garlic clove.
2. Add shrimps in the mixture and make 2 equal balls.
3. Flatten the balls and fry in a skillet for 8 minutes, flipping once halfway through cooking.
4. When cooked, transfer to a serving plate.
5. Serve and enjoy!
Serving Suggestions: Serve with lime wedges on top.
Variation Tip: Sriracha sauce can be replaced with hot chili sauce.
Nutritional Information per Serving:
Calories: 312 | Fat: 14.8g|Sat Fat: 4g|Carbs: 23.7g|Fiber: 1.9g|Sugar: 3.1g|Protein: 19.8g

Refreshing Thai Iced Tea (Cha Yen)

Prep Time: 15 minutes.
Cook Time: 1 minute.
Serves: 1

Ingredients:
• 1 tablespoon Thai black tea
• 1 cup hot, scalding water
• 2 teaspoon condensed milk, sweetened
• 2 tablespoons evaporated milk (plus some more to sprinkle on top)
• 2 teaspoons sugar
• 1 cup ice, crushed

Preparation:
1. Bring water to a boil.
2. Fill your tea sock with 1 tablespoon of Thai black tea. It is easiest to place your tea sock in a bowl or large cup to steep the tea.
3. Pour 1 cup of boiling water into the tea sock and gently force it in and out to steep the tea and absorb all of the flavors. Steep the tea for a few minutes or until it has turned a pleasant dark color.
4. Pour 1 glass of hot tea into a fresh cup.
5. Stir in 2 teaspoons of sugar and 2 teaspoons of sweetened condensed milk.
6. Then whisk in 2 teaspoons of evaporated milk, continuing to stir until all is thoroughly combined.
7. Optional - A good Thai iced tea should have some froth or bubbles on top, so take two pitchers and spill the tea from one to the other with a bit of elevation. You might do it differently, but it's a lot of fun!
8. Fill a cup all the way to the top with crushed ice.
9. The gentry Pour your hot tea mixture over the ice in a cup.
10. Drizzle some more evaporated milk on top of your Thai iced tea to add a final creamy touch.
11. With the addition of a straw, you're able to slurp it down!

Serving Suggestion: Serve chilled with some ice cubes if you want it to be more refreshing.
Variation Tip: Add some shredded coconut on top.
Nutritional Information Per Serving:
Calories 186 | Fat 0g |Sodium 16mg | Carbs 48g | Fiber 2g | Sugar 43g | Protein 1g

Traditional Thai Rice Pudding

Prep Time: 15 minutes.
Cook Time: 25 to 30 minutes.
Serves: 4

Ingredients:
• 2 cups Thai sweet rice (known as sticky or glutinous rice)
• 3 ½ cups water
• ½ teaspoon salt
• 1 can coconut milk
• ¾ cup palm sugar
• 1 teaspoon vanilla
• 1 teaspoon cinnamon
• ¼ teaspoon nutmeg
• ¼ teaspoon ground cloves

Preparation:
1. Take a large-sized pot with a lid and add 2 cups of water.
2. Add the rice and let it soak for about 10 minutes.
3. Add 1 and a ½ cups of water and salt.
4. Stir well.
5. Place the mixture over high heat and bring it to a boil.
6. Lower the heat to medium-low just as it starts to boil and partially cover the pot with a lid.
7. Boil it as such for 15-20 minutes until the water has been absorbed.
8. Remove the heat and let the rice steam for 10 minutes (by keeping the lid on).
9. Remove the lid and add coconut milk and keep stirring well until fully mixed.
10. Turn the heat to low and simmer it.
11. Add ¾ cup of sugar.
12. Add vanilla, nutmeg, cinnamon, and cloves.
13. Taste it for sweetness and season to your preference.
14. Eventually, the rice will absorb the coconut milk and turn into a nice rice pudding.
15. Garnish with some cinnamon, crushed peanuts, star anise, and serve!

Serving Suggestion: Serve with a topping of ice cream if desired.
Variation Tip: Add Banana Blossom/Basil/Oyster Sauce during or after cooking for an additional flavorful punch.
Nutritional Information Per Serving:
Calories 135 | Fat 5g |Sodium 84mg | Carbs 20g | Fiber 1g | Sugar 1g | Protein 4g

Thai Mango Pudding

Preparation Time: 15 minutes
Servings: 10
Ingredients:
- 4 mangoes
- 1 cup water
- ½ cup white sugar
- 1½ cups coconut milk
- 4 tablespoons gelatin powder

Preparation:
1. In a food processor, add mangos and pulse to form a smooth puree.
2. Remove the puree from the food processor and transfer to a bowl. Add coconut milk and mix well.
3. In a bowl, add gelatin powder, sugar, and boiled water and stir well.
4. Now mix together the mango and the gelatin mixture.
5. Serve the mixture in serving glasses after cooled.
6. Enjoy!

Serving Suggestions: Top it with whipped cream before serving.
Variation Tip: Coconut sugar can also be used.
Nutritional Information per Serving:
Calories: 431 | Fat: 32g|Sat Fat: 28g|Carbs: 37.4g|Fiber: 5.1g|Sugar: 32.8g|Protein: 6.5g

Classic Thai-style Banana in Coconut Milk

Preparation Time: 10 minutes
Cooking Time: 10 minutes
Servings: 4
Ingredients:
- 3 cups coconut milk
- 2 tablespoons sugar
- 4 bananas, sliced
- Salt, to taste

Preparation:
1. In a saucepan, add coconut milk and bring to a boil.
2. Then add the banana slices in the pan and reduce heat to simmer for about 5 minutes.
3. Season with sugar and salt.
Serve in serving glasses. Enjoy! **Serving Suggestions:** Top with shredded coconut before serving.
Variation Tip: You can also add honey to enhance taste.
Nutritional Information per Serving:
Calories: 542 | Fat: 43.3g|Sat Fat: 38.2g|Carbs: 42.9g|Fiber: 7g|Sugar: 26.4g|Protein: 5.4g

A Fruity Bowl

Prep Time: 15 minutes.
Serves: 4
Ingredients:
- 2 fresh ripe mangoes
- 2 cups pineapple chunks
- Fresh pineapple tips
- 1 sliced banana
- 1-2 cups fresh papaya slice up into cubes
- Kiwi fruits sliced up into cubes
- Berries sliced up into cubes
- 2 cups fresh seedless grapes sliced up in half
- ¼ cup coconut milk
- 2 tablespoons lime juice
- 3-4 tablespoons sugar (depending on your preference)

Preparation:
1. Slice up the listed fruits except for the contrasting red ones (raspberries, dried cranberries, and strawberries) and add them to a mixing bowl.
2. Drizzle a bit of lime juice on top and stir well.
3. Sprinkle some sugar and stir well.
4. Chill in your fridge for 30 minutes.
5. Before serving the salad, add a bit of coconut milk and give the mixture a stir.
6. Taste it and adjust the sweetness accordingly.
7. Top it up with some raspberries, dried cranberries, and strawberries.
8. Serve!

Serving Suggestion: Serve with a topping of Ice Cream!
Variation Tip: Add some shredded coconut on top.
Nutritional Information Per Serving:
Calories 260 | Fat 1g |Sodium 30mg | Carbs 66g | Fiber 4g | Sugar 59g | Protein 2g

Thai-style Banana Spring Rolls

Preparation Time: 10 minutes
Cooking Time: 4 minutes
Servings: 6
Ingredients:
- 6 spring roll wrappers
- 3 tablespoons palm sugar
- 1½ tablespoons butter
- 3 bananas, halved
- 1½ tablespoons oil

Preparation:
1. In each wrapper, add banana half and ½ tablespoon sugar and fold the wrappers with water.
2. In a pan, add butter and oil. Then add the spring roll and fry each side for 2 minutes.
3. When cooked, remove and serve.

Serving Suggestions: Top with icing sugar before serving.
Variation Tip: You can add some cinnamon too.
Nutritional Information per Serving:
Calories: 357 | Fat: 23.7|Sat Fat: 8.5g|Carbs: 34g|Fiber: 2.1g|Sugar: 9.1g|Protein: 3.9g

Tasty Steamed Banana Cake

Preparation Time: 5 minutes
Cooking Time: 30 minutes
Servings: 2
Ingredients:
- 1 banana
- 1 tablespoon coconut flour
- ½ cup grated coconut meat
- ¼ cup rice flour
- ½ cup sugar
- ¼ cup coconut milk

Preparation:
1. In a bowl, mash the banana.
2. Mix in the coconut milk, rice flour, half grated coconut meat, coconut flour, and sugar to make a batter.
3. Then pour the batter in a cake mould and steam for about 30 minutes.
4. When cooked, take out.
5. Then add the remaining grated coconut meat on the top.
6. Serve and enjoy!

Serving Suggestions: Top with banana slices before serving.
Variation Tip: You can also add honey to enhance taste.
Nutritional Information per Serving:
Calories: 470 | Fat: 14.3g|Sat Fat: 12.4g|Carbs: 88.2g|Fiber: 4.8g|Sugar: 59.7g|Protein: 3.5g

Thai-inspired Grilled Pineapples

Preparation Time: 5 minutes
Cooking Time: 6 minutes
Servings: 2
Ingredients:
- ½ pineapple, sliced
- 1½ tablespoons butter
- 1 tablespoon palm sugar
- ½ tablespoon coconut, grated
- 1½ tablespoons lemon juice

Preparation:
1. In a pan, add butter and heat to melt. Then add the pineapple slices.
2. Sprinkle palm sugar over and drizzle with lemon juice. Cook for about 3 minutes per side.
3. When cooked, remove and add grated coconut on the top.
4. Serve and enjoy!

Serving Suggestions: Serve with steamed rice.
Variation Tip: Pineapple juice can be used instead of lemon juice.
Nutritional Information per Serving:
Calories: 323 | Fat: 32.5g|Sat Fat: 20.8g|Carbs: 8.5g|Fiber: 0.9g|Sugar: 6.9g|Protein: 0.9g

Aromatic Coconut Pudding

Preparation Time: 10 minutes
Cooking Time: 35 minutes
Servings: 6
Ingredients:
- 4 eggs
- 1 teaspoon vanilla essence
- ¾ tablespoons brown sugar
- 1 tablespoon all-purpose flour
- ½ cup grated coconut
- 1 cup coconut milk
- Icing sugar, to taste

Preparation:
1. Before cooking, heat the baking oven to 260 degrees F. Prepare a baking dish and use cooking spray or butter to grease.
2. In a large bowl, whisk eggs and add sugar.
3. Then add in grated coconut, vanilla essence, and coconut milk. Whisk together.
4. Transfer the mixture to a baking dish and bake in the preheated oven for 35 minutes.
5. Remove from the oven and add icing sugar on the top to serve.
6. Enjoy!

Serving Suggestions: Top with whipped cream before serving.
Variation Tip: You can use coconut sugar instead of brown sugar.
Nutritional Information per Serving:
Calories: 174 | Fat: 14.7g|Sat Fat: 11.3g|Carbs: 7g|Fiber: 1.5g|Sugar: 4.5g|Protein: 5g

Awesome Thai Banana Custard

Prep Time: 15 minutes.
Cook Time: 60 minutes.
Serves: 4
Ingredients:
- 1 cup coconut milk
- ⅓ cup sugar
- 2 whole eggs
- 1 ripe banana
- 1 teaspoon coconut flavoring

- Oil for grease
Preparation:
1. Preheat your oven to a temperature of 350 degrees Fahrenheit.
2. Prepare 4-6 ramekins and grease them up with a bit of oil.
3. Add your coconut milk, eggs, sugar, banana, and coconut flavorings into a blender and mix well for 30 seconds.
4. Pour the mixture into your ramekins, making sure to fill them up by ¾.
5. Add the ramekins to a flat-bottomed glass dish and fill the dish partway with water (about ½ the height of your ramekins).
6. Bake for about 60 minutes until a nice custardy texture appears.
7. Serve your ramekins hot or chilled.
8. If needed, then sprinkle a bit of sugar or shredded coconut on top.

Serving Suggestion: Serve with a topping of ice cream for more taste.
Variation Tip: Add some shredded coconut on top.
Nutritional Information Per Serving:
Calories 243 | Fat 6g |Sodium 162mg | Carbs 42g | Fiber 3g | Sugar 24g | Protein 8g

Scrumptious Tropical Fruit Salad

Preparation Time: 7 minutes
Servings: 3
Ingredients:
- ½ cup fresh pineapple cubes
- ½ cup mango, sliced
- ½ star fruit, peeled and sliced
- 2 tablespoons coconut milk
- 1½ tablespoons coconut sugar
- ½ banana, sliced
- ½ cup lychee fruit
- 1 cup strawberries
- ½ tablespoon lime juice

Preparation:
1. In a bowl, mix together lime juice, sugar, and coconut milk.
2. In another bowl, add pineapple, star fruit, banana, strawberries, mango slices, and lychee and mix well.
3. Toss together the coconut milk mixture with the fruits until well coated.
4. Serve and enjoy!

Serving Suggestions: Serve with berries on the top.
Variation Tip: You can also use brown sugar.
Nutritional Information per Serving:
Calories: 277 | Fat: 2.8g|Sat Fat: 2.2g|Carbs: 55.7g|Fiber: 2.8g|Sugar: 11.2g|Protein: 3.4g

Easy Thai Strawberry Cheesecake Rolled Ice Cream

Preparation Time: 10 minutes + 6 hours for frozen
Cooking Time: 4 minutes
Servings: 4
Ingredients:
• 2 cups cream
• 6 strawberries, diced
• 4 tablespoons cream cheese
• 1 cup condensed milk
• 4 tablespoons crushed graham crackers
Preparation:
1. Mix together the condensed milk and cream in a large baking tray.
2. Add strawberries, graham crackers, and cream cheese in the bowl.
3. Then break all the ingredients into small chunks to combine well.
4. Arrange the prepared tray in the freezer overnight or for at least 6 hours.
5. Use an offset spatula to roll the rice cream into itself to spiral.
6. Add whipped cream on the top to serve!
Serving Suggestions: Serve with strawberry slices on the top.
Variation Tip: You can also add strawberry syrup for an even better taste.
Nutritional Information per Serving:
Calories: 386 | Fat: 17.4g|Sat Fat: 10.6g|Carbs: 51.1g|Fiber: 0.5g|Sugar: 46.6g|Protein: 8.3g

Savory Thai Mango Cake (Khek Ma-Muang)

Preparation Time: 5 minutes
Cooking Time: 30 minutes
Servings: 4
Ingredients:

• 3 eggs
• ½ tablespoon sweetened dried coconut
• 1 teaspoon baking powder
• 1 tablespoon coconut oil
• 1 cup diced mangoes
• ½ cup sugar
• ½ cup all-purpose flour
• ½ teaspoon vanilla extract
• ⅛ teaspoon salt
Preparation:
1. Before cooking, heat the baking oven to 325 degrees F. Prepare a cake pan and grease.
2. In a large bowl, beat eggs and add sugar. Whisk well.
3. Beat in all-purpose flour, baking powder, vanilla extract, salt, and coconut oil.
4. In a blender, blend half the diced mangos to form a puree.
5. Mix the puree and batter and beat well.
6. Then bake the mixture in the preheated oven for about 30 minutes.
7. Remove from the oven and add dried coconut and the remaining mango cubes on the top.
8. Serve and enjoy!
Serving Suggestions: Add whipped cream on the top before serving.
Variation Tip: Vanilla extract can be replaced with coconut extract.
Nutritional Information per Serving:
Calories: 278 | Fat: 9.3g|Sat Fat: 6.1g|Carbs: 44.9g|Fiber: 1.7g|Sugar: 31.3g|Protein: 6.3g

Lovely Pink Milk (Thai Nom Yen)

Prep Time: 5 minutes.
Serves: 4
Ingredients:
• 1 tablespoon sala syrup
• 2 tablespoons condensed milk
• ¾ cup of milk
• 8 optional ice cubes
Preparation:
1. Take a sizable bottle. For an extra chilled experience, place it in the freezer for 5-10 minutes before serving. After that, fill it with ice (optional).
2. Combine the sala syrup and condensed milk in a mixing bowl.
3. Pour in your milk, stir all together, and serve right away.
Serving Suggestion: Serve chilled with some ice cubes if you want it to be more refreshing.
Variation Tip: Add some shredded coconut on top
Nutritional Information Per Serving:
Calories 174 | Fat 12g |Sodium 43mg | Carbs 16g | Fiber 0g | Sugar 4g | Protein 2g

Thai Basil Shaved Ice Dessert

Preparation Time: 10 minutes
Servings: 2
Ingredients:
- 2 tablespoons basil seeds, soaked
- 1½ tablespoons croutons
- 2 teaspoons condensed milk
- 2 cups shaved ice
- 6 tablespoons raspberry syrup

Preparation:
1. In a dessert bowl, add a layer of basil seeds, ice, and croutons.
2. Then drizzle with honey and condensed milk on top.
3. Serve and enjoy!
Serving Suggestions: Top with raspberries before serving.
Variation Tip: You can also use blueberry syrup.
Nutritional Information per Serving:
Calories: 374 | Fat: 15.1g|Sat Fat: 11.4g|Carbs: 59.5g|Fiber: 1g|Sugar: 51.5g|Protein: 3.9g

Simple Mango Ice Cream

Preparation Time: 15 minutes + 8 hours for frozen
Servings: 12
Ingredients:
- 4 mangoes, sliced
- 6 tablespoons coconut milk
- 2 cups whipping cream

- 2 cups white sugar
- 2 teaspoons lemon juice

Preparation:
1. In an ice cream maker, add coconut milk, whipping cream, sugar, lemon juice, and mango slices and process according to the manufacturer's instructions.
2. Transfer the mixture in an airtight container.
3. Put in a freezer for about 8 hours.
4. Serve and enjoy!
Serving Suggestions: Top with mango slices before serving.
Variation Tip: Almond milk can be used instead of coconut milk.
Nutritional Information per Serving:
Calories: 268 | Fat: 8.4g|Sat Fat: 5.6g|Carbs: 51.1g|Fiber: 2g|Sugar: 48.9g|Protein: 1.5g

Delicious Mango Rice Pudding (Kao Niew Ma Muang)

Prep Time: 15 minutes.
Cook Time: 5 minutes.
Serves: 4
Ingredients:
- 2 medium mangos
- 3 teaspoons gelatin
- ½ cup hot water
- ⅓ cup white sugar
- 1 cup coconut milk

Preparation:
1. Scoop out the flesh off your mangoes fruit and place them in a food processor.
2. Blitz them until a mango puree form.
3. Leave it be.
4. Take a saucepan and place it over medium heat.
5. Add water and allow it to heat up.
6. Remove the heat and keep stirring it while adding the gelatin to the surface.
7. Stir well to ensure that no lumps are formed.
8. Add sugar to the water/gelatin mix and stir well.
9. Add the mixture to your mango puree.
10. Add coconut milk.
11. Blitz well until the ingredients are combined well.
12. Pour the mixture into your dessert bowls.
13. Allow them to chill for 2 hours.
14. Serve with some fresh fruit!
Serving Suggestion: Serve with a topping of Ice Cream for added flavor!
Variation Tip: Add some shredded coconut on top.
Nutritional Information Per Serving:
Calories 789 | Fat 30g |Sodium 1346mg | Carbs 123g | Fiber 4g | Sugar 71g | Protein 7g

Simple Lemongrass Drink

Prep Time: 10 minutes.
Cook Time: 10 minutes
Serves: 1
Ingredients:
• 5 big lemon grass stalks
• 2 ½ cups water
• ¼ – ½ cup sugar
• Pinch of salt
• Lime Juice
Preparation:
1. Thinly slice the lemon grass.
2. Simmer for 7-8 minutes in a saucepan with the water.
3. Stir in the sugar to dissolve it. Allow cooling before straining the lemon grass.
4. Serve over a large amount of ice.
Serving Suggestion: Serve chilled with some ice cubes if you want it to be more refreshing.
Variation Tip: Add some shredded coconut on top!
Nutritional Information Per Serving:
Calories 395 | Fat 4g |Sodium 37mg | Carbs 95g | Fiber 20g | Sugar 66g | Protein 7g

Authentic Iced Coffee (Oliang)

Prep Time: 15 minutes.
Cook Time: Nil
Serves: 4
Ingredients:
• 2 tablespoons Oliang powder
• 300ml water
• 3 heaping tablespoons sugar
• 3 tablespoons sweetened condensed milk
• ice, crushed
Preparation:

1. Fill the muslin filter halfway with Oliang powder.
2. Bring water to a boil and slowly pour it through the muslin filter into a clean tub.
3. Pour the liquid two more times through the same muslin filter.
4. The coffee is ready when all of the liquid has been drained from the filter for the third time.
5. Stir in the sugar and condensed milk until the sugar dissolves.
6. Place the mixture in the freezer for about 15 minutes to cool.
7. Pour the coffee into a tumbler over crushed ice, leaving space for milk or cream on top.
Serving Suggestion: Serve chilled with some ice cubes if you want it to be more refreshing.
Variation Tip: Add some shredded coconut on top!
Nutritional Information Per Serving:
Calories 446 | Fat 26g |Sodium 162mg | Carbs 49g | Fiber 0g | Sugar 36g | Protein 5g

Thai-inspired Dragon Fruit Vodka Cocktail

Preparation Time: 10 minutes
Servings: 4
Ingredients:
• 2 cups dragon fruit
• 2 teaspoons honey
• ¾ cup vodka
• Juice of 4 limes
• 2 blood oranges
• ¼ cup orange liquor
Preparation:
1. In a blender, blend together the dragon fruit, lime juice, and blood orange until smooth.
2. Then add in honey, orange liquor, and vodka. Mix well.
3. Remove from the blender.
4. Add the crushed ice on the top. Serve and enjoy!
Serving Suggestions: Top with mint leaves before serving.
Variation Tip: Maple syrup can be used instead of honey.
Nutritional Information per Serving:
Calories: 204 | Fat: 1.2g|Sat Fat: 0.6g|Carbs: 27.2 |Fiber: 4.4g|Sugar: 18.6g|Protein: 1.6g

Awesome Thai Bubble Tea (Boba Tea)

Prep Time: 5 minutes.
Cook Time: 5 minutes
Serves: 1
Ingredients:
To Make the Thai Tea:
- 13 cups (180ml) Pantai Thai Tea Blend
- 3 quarts (720 mL) of water
For the Boba & completing the drink:
- ½ cup (100g) granulated sugar
- ½ cup (120ml) tapioca pearls that have been dried
- ½ cup (120ml) milk, half-and-half, or another creamer (some people use coconut milk, heavy cream, or sweetened condensed milk)

Preparation:
1. Bring the water to a boil before adding the Thai tea mix and sugar. Stir until the sugar is fully dissolved. Tea should be gently boiled for about 3 minutes. Take the pan off the heat.
2. Enable the tea to steep for at least 30 minutes before serving. The stronger the tea flavor, the better Thai tea tastes.
3. Set aside the Thai tea to cool (we prefer to strain through a traditional re-useable cloth filter to remove any sediment). You can make this ahead of time and store the Thai tea in the refrigerator. Chill completely before serving.
4. Cook tapioca pearls according to package directions; see Note 1 for instructions on cooking the boba we purchased.
5. Divide the warm tapioca pearls into two (16-ounce) glasses. Fill the two glasses halfway with cold tea.
6. Fill with glass with around ¼ cup milk (or preferred creamer). Enjoy with a straw after you've stirred it up.

Serving Suggestion: Serve chilled with some ice cubes if you want it to be more refreshing.
Variation Tip: Add some shredded coconut on top.
Nutritional Information Per Serving:
Calories 449 | Fat 1g |Sodium 49mg | Carbs 111g | Fiber 1g | Sugar 75g | Protein 0g

Conclusion

Thailand is the most acclaimed nation in the whole world for its cooking. Traversing from the southern landmass toward the northern regions, the nation offers a varied mix of madly flavorful food. Thai food is not the only cuisine to have been changed in the excursion across seas. Various vegetarian Thai foods are loved across the world. You, in particular, would enjoy cooking your vegetarian food with the Thai flavors inserted in them.

The different flavors utilized in Thai cooking have a tremendous measure of astounding properties that soundly affect our general wellbeing. This cookbook incorporates 80 healthy Thai recipes covering poultry, snacks, noodle, curries, salads, seafood, and everything in between that you can undoubtedly make at home without the help of any kind.

I would like to thank you for purchasing and downloading my book. I really do hope that you had a pleasant time with my book and enjoyed reading it.

I bid you farewell and hope that your journey into the world of Thai cuisine may turn out to be a huge success!

Stay healthy and stay safe.

Appendix Measurement Conversion Chart

WEIGHT EQUIVALENTS

US STANDARD	METRIC (APPROXIMATE)
1 ounce	28 g
2 ounces	57 g
5 ounces	142 g
10 ounces	284 g
15 ounces	425 g
16 ounces (1 pound)	455 g
1.5pounds	680 g
2pounds	907 g

VOLUME EQUIVALENTS (DRY)

US STANDARD	METRIC (APPROXIMATE)
⅛ teaspoon	0.5 mL
¼ teaspoon	1 mL
½ teaspoon	2 mL
¾ teaspoon	4 mL
1 teaspoon	5 mL
1 tablespoon	15 mL
¼ cup	59 mL
½ cup	118 mL
¾ cup	177 mL
1 cup	235 mL
2 cups	475 mL
3 cups	700 mL
4 cups	1 L

TEMPERATURES EQUIVALENTS

FAHRENHEIT(F)	CELSIUS (C) (APPROXIMATE)
225 °F	107 °C
250 °F	120 °C
275 °F	135 °C
300 °F	150 °C
325 °F	160 °C
350 °F	180 °C
375 °F	190 °C
400 °F	205 °C
425 °F	220 °C
450 °F	235 °C
475 °F	245 °C
500 °F	260 °C

VOLUME EQUIVALENTS (LIQUID)

US STANDARD	US STANDARD (OUNCES)	METRIC (APPROXIMATE)
2 tablespoons	1 fl.oz	30 mL
¼ cup	2 fl.oz	60 mL
½ cup	4 fl.oz	120 mL
1 cup	8 fl.oz	240 mL
1½ cup	12 fl.oz	355 mL
2 cups or 1 pint	16 fl.oz	475 mL
4 cups or 1 quart	32 fl.oz	1 L
1 gallon	128 fl.oz	4 L

Printed in Great Britain
by Amazon

28444185R00044